CHOCOLATE COOKBOOK

A Decadent Collection of Morning Pastries and Nostalgic Sweets

(Chocolate Cake Cookbook - the Magic to Create Incredible Flavor)

Stuart Grantham

Published by Alex Howard

© **Stuart Grantham**

All Rights Reserved

Chocolate Cookbook: A Decadent Collection of Morning Pastries and Nostalgic Sweets (Chocolate Cake Cookbook - the Magic to Create Incredible Flavor)

ISBN 978-1-990169-13-7

All rights reserved. No part of this guide may be reproduced in any form without permission in writing from the publisher except in the case of brief quotations embodied in critical articles or reviews.

Legal & Disclaimer

The information contained in this book is not designed to replace or take the place of any form of medicine or professional medical advice. The information in this book has been provided for educational and entertainment purposes only.

The information contained in this book has been compiled from sources deemed reliable, and it is accurate to the best of the Author's knowledge; however, the Author cannot guarantee its accuracy and validity and cannot be held liable for any errors or omissions. Changes are periodically made to this book. You must consult your doctor or get professional medical advice before using any of the suggested remedies, techniques, or information in this book.

Table of contents

PART 1 1

CHAPTER 1: HISTORY OF CHOCOLATE 2

    INITIAL DISCOVERY OF THE CACAO TREE 2
    MAYANS AND CHOCOLATE 4
    HOW MAYANS PREPARED CHOCOLATE 4
    AZTECS AND CHOCOLATE 5
    EUROPEANS ARE INTRODUCED TO CHOCOLATE 7
    CHOCOLATE MOVES TO FRANCE 7
    CHOCOLATE AND ENGLAND 8
    THE SHAPE OF CHOCOLATE 9
    CHOCOLATE AND CONTROVERSY 10

CHAPTER 2: CHOCOLATE INFORMATION AND INTERESTING FACTS ABOUT CHOCOLATE 11

    THE CACAO TREE 11
    HOW CHOCOLATE IS MADE 13
    INTERESTING INFORMATION ABOUT CHOCOLATE 15

CHAPTER 3: TYPES OF CHOCOLATE 18

    WHITE CHOCOLATE 18
    MILK CHOCOLATE 19
    BITTER CHOCOLATE 20
    DARK CHOCOLATE 22
    SEMISWEET CHOCOLATE 23

CHAPTER 4: CHOCOLATE AND HEALTH - HEALTH EFFECTS OF CHOCOLATE . 26

    WHICH CHOCOLATES HAVE HEALTH BENEFITS? 26
    THE HISTORY OF CHOCOLATE AND HEALTH 27
    ANTIOXIDANTS 29
    HEART HEALTH 29
    ENERGY 30
    MOOD 31

Myths Surrounding Chocolate And Health 31
Beauty 33

CHAPTER 5: CHOCOLATE RECIPE VARIATIONS 35

Chocolate Cake Recipes 35
Chocolate Candy Recipes 37
Chocolate Chip Cookie Recipes 39
Chocolate Covered Recipes 41
Chocolate Desserts 42
Chocolate Truffle Recipes 43
Chocolate Drink Recipes 44
Chocolate Soufflé Recipes 45
Chocolate Covered Strawberries 46
Diabetic Chocolate Recipes 47
Lactose Free Chocolate Recipes 48

CHAPTER 6: CHOCOLATE CAKE RECIPES 50

Black Magic Cake 51
German Sweet Chocolate Cake 52
Black Forest Cake 54
Mocha Layer Cake 56
Extreme Chocolate Cake 57
Chapter 7: Chocolate Candy Recipes 59
Kentucky Bourbon Balls 60
Maple Walnut Fudge 61
Caramel Clusters With Nuts 62
Dark Chocolate Truffles 63
Tiger Butter Candy 64

CHAPTER 8: CHOCOLATE CHIP COOKIE RECIPES 65

Triple Chocolate Chip Cookies 66
White Chocolate Chip Oatmeal Cookies 68
Chocolate Pileup Cookies 69
Chocolate Mint Brownie Cookies 71
Ideal Chocolate Chip Cookies 73

CHAPTER 9: CHOCOLATE COVERED RECIPES 74

Chocolate Covered Graham Crackers 75
Chocolate Covered Potato Chips 76
White Chocolate Covered Pretzels 77
Chocolate Covered Cheesecake Bites 78
Chocolate Covered Frozen Bananas 80

CHAPTER 10: CHOCOLATE DESSERTS 81

Chocolate Mousse 82
French Silk Chocolate Pie 83
Chocolate Pudding 84
Dark Chocolate Cake 85
Chocolate Cheesecake 87

CHAPTER 11: CHOCOLATE DRINK RECIPES 88

Thick Chocolate Shake 89
Chocolate Martini 90
Chocolate Covered Cherry Shooters 91
Chilled Hot Chocolate 92
Candy Cane Cocoa 93

CHAPTER 12: CHOCOLATE SOUFFLÉ RECIPES 94

Easy Chocolate Soufflé 95
Mexican Chocolate Soufflés 97
Chocolate Liquor Soufflés 98
Dark Chocolate Soufflé 100
Mini Chocolate Soufflés 102
Chapter 13: Chocolate Truffle Recipes 103
Easy Chocolate Truffles *104*
Luscious Chocolate Truffles 105
Chocolate Truffles 106
White Chocolate Truffles 107
Easy Chocolate Cookie Truffles 108

CHAPTER 14: CHOCOLATE COVERED STRAWBERRIES 109

Divine Chocolate Coated Strawberries 110
Chocolate Covered Strawberries 111
Creamy Chocolate Covered Strawberries 113

CHOCOLATE COVERED STRAWBERRIES 114
CHOCOLATE DIPPED STRAWBERRIES 115
CHAPTER 15: DIABETIC CHOCOLATE RECIPES 117
CHOCOLATE BANANA MOUSSE 118
CHOCOLATE BALLS 119
SUGAR FREE CHOCOLATE NUT CLUSTERS 120
SUGAR FREE CHOCOLATE BUTTER CREAMS 121
BITTERSWEET CHOCOLATE SAUCE 123

CHAPTER 16: LACTOSE FREE CHOCOLATE RECIPES 124

CHOCOLATE WITH CHOCOLATE CHIP PANCAKES 125
DAIRY FREE CHOCOLATE PUDDING 126
LACTOSE FREE CHOCOLATE CAKE 127
DAIRY FREE CHOCOLATE CHIP COOKIES 128
DAIRY FREE HOT CHOCOLATE 129

PART 2 130

CHOCOLATE CAKE RECIPES 131

BLACK MAGIC CAKE 132
GERMAN SWEET CHOCOLATE CAKE 133
BLACK FOREST CAKE 135
MOCHA LAYER CAKE 137
EXTREME CHOCOLATE CAKE 139

CHOCOLATE CANDY RECIPES 141

KENTUCKY BOURBON BALLS 141
MAPLE WALNUT FUDGE 142
CARAMEL CLUSTERS WITH NUTS 143
DARK CHOCOLATE TRUFFLES 144
TIGER BUTTER CANDY 145

CHOCOLATE CHIP COOKIE RECIPES 146

TRIPLE CHOCOLATE CHIP COOKIES 146
WHITE CHOCOLATE CHIP OATMEAL COOKIES 148
CHOCOLATE PILEUP COOKIES 149
CHOCOLATE MINT BROWNIE COOKIES 151

Ideal Chocolate Chip Cookies	153
Chocolate Covered Recipes	153
Chocolate Covered Graham Crackers	154
Chocolate Covered Potato Chips	155
White Chocolate Covered Pretzels	156
Chocolate Covered Cheesecake Bites	157
Chocolate Covered Frozen Bananas	159

CHOCOLATE DESSERTS 160

Chocolate Mousse	160
French Silk Chocolate Pie	162
Chocolate Pudding	163
Dark Chocolate Cake	164
Chocolate Cheesecake	165

CHOCOLATE DRINK RECIPES 166

Thick Chocolate Shake	166
Chocolate Martini	167
Chocolate Covered Cherry Shooters	168
Chilled Hot Chocolate	169
Candy Cane Cocoa	170

CHOCOLATE SOUFFLE RECIPES 171

Easy Chocolate Soufflé	171
Mexican Chocolate Soufflés	173
Chocolate Liquor Soufflés	174
Dark Chocolate Soufflé	176
Mini Chocolate Soufflés	178
Chocolate Truffle Recipes	179
Easy Chocolate Truffles	179
Luscious Chocolate Truffles	181
Chocolate Truffles	182
White Chocolate Truffles	183
Easy Chocolate Cookie Truffles	184

CHOCOLATE COVERED STRAWBERRIES 185

Divine Chocolate Coated Strawberries	185

CHOCOLATE COVERED STRAWBERRIES 187
CREAMY CHOCOLATE COVERED STRAWBERRIES... 188
Chocolate Covered Strawberries (2).. *189*

Part 1

Chapter 1: History Of Chocolate

The history of chocolate has roots in ancient cultures. Chocolate comes from the cacao tree, which has origins in the warm and humid climate of South America. It has a tender, fragile trunk that must be handled with caution, and its bright glossy leaves blend with a beautiful show of blossoms. The blossoms give way to large, pineapple-sized pods that hold juicy, fleshy pulp and approximately forty cacao beans. The cacao pods are carefully harvested and prepared for use in a variety of foods and drinks, and they have been used for many purposes throughout the centuries.

Initial Discovery Of The Cacao Tree

The history of chocolate began when monkeys discovered the delights within the pods of the cacao tree. They loved to eat the fleshy pulp, which has a flavour that is similar to apricots. Monkeys did not like the bitter seeds, however, and they spit them out on the ground, allowing more cacao trees to sprout.
When the ancient people saw what the monkeys were eating, they decided to try the pods out for themselves. They originally only ate the pulps but left the beans on the ground. At some point in the history of chocolate, ancient people, possibly the Olmecs, found that roasting the beans lessened the bitter characteristics

while enhancing the chocolate flavour. It appears that the cacao beans then became a staple of the Olmecs' diet, and it is possible that they were the ones that named the tree kakawa, now known as cacao.

Mayans And Chocolate

Mayans are the first people documented in the history of chocolate that incorporated cacao beans into various aspects of their culture. Archaeologists have found pottery pieces that depict images of gods battling over the beans of the cacao tree. There have also been remnants of cacao beans found in goblets, and texts have discussed the importance of cacao in Mayan culture.

They used the cacao pod as a symbol of fertility and life, and it was an important part of religious ceremonies. The Mayans believed that gods had sent it to them, and they held an annual celebration in honour of the gift. During the ceremony, they sacrificed a dog with hair the colour of cacao, and they gave offerings of cacao and incense.

How Mayans Prepared Chocolate

Mayans would combine the cacao beans with several other ingredients to create a variety of drinks and foods. They harvested the cacao pods and carefully extracted the beans. They would then place the beans in a pit in the ground and cover them with leaves. After the beans had fermented, they would roast them over a fire before grinding them into a powder. The powder was sometimes mixed with maize, which was another important source of food for the Mayans. They also mixed it with vanilla, chili peppers and honey.

One of the most documented uses for chocolate in Mayan culture was as a drink. The chocolate was poured back and forth while being mixed with a beater until it became frothy. In addition to using it in religious ceremonies, they drank it as a herbal remedy and as a way to administer other medicines.

The Mayans also used cacao beans as currency. They often traded it for cloth or ceremonial feathers, and the beans were used as payment for items such as rabbits, eggs and even slaves.

Aztecs And Chocolate

The history of chocolate did not alter much after the Aztecs conquered the Mayans. The Aztecs regarded chocolate in much the same way as the Mayan Indians. They believed that one of their gods, Quetzalcoatl, stole a cacao tree and delivered it to them to cultivate. Quetzalcoatl was banished by the other gods because he had shared the divine plant with the people.

The beans were used to make a drink that was similar to what the Mayans consumed. King Montezuma reportedly drank as many as fifty goblets of chocolate each day and many times each goblet was used only once.

The Aztec warriors consumed chocolate to gain strength and energy, and it was used to cure a variety of ailments. They believed that it had powers to heal and that one could gain wisdom, knowledge and power by eating or drinking chocolate. It was even thought to be a powerful aphrodisiac.

When Spaniards later added their observations about the history of chocolate, they noted that the flowers of the cacao tree were used in baths, and many of the priests and wealthy citizens consumed chocolate regularly for its purported health benefits. Aztecs had no knowledge of sugar, but they added chili peppers, spices and honey to chocolate to make it more palatable.

Europeans Are Introduced To Chocolate

Up to this point in the history of chocolate, no European had ever seen or tasted cacao beans. When Columbus travelled near Mexico, he came across a canoe of Indians that were carrying the beans to trade. He dismissed the cacao beans as unimportant, but his son Ferdinand noticed how the Indians seemed to value them highly. While Columbus took some cacao beans back with him to Spain, they were not considered to be noteworthy.

When Hernán Cortés arrived in Mexico, Montezuma believed that Cortés was Quetzalcoatl returning as promised. He eagerly handed over gold, which prompted the Spaniards to conquer the Aztecs. Cortés was not impressed by the chocolate drink that the Aztecs consumed, but he was interested in the possibility of using cacao beans as currency. He began a cacao tree plantation and may even be credited with bringing the tree to West Africa.

Chocolate Moves To France

In 1660, Maria Theresa, a Spanish princess, moved to the court of King Louis XIV. She brought a trunk of cacao beans with her as well as her chefs that were trained in preparing her chocolate drinks.

The wedding guests received a cup of hot chocolate, and the drink became well-known and appreciated rather quickly, which made the wedding ceremony a turning point in the history of chocolate. Even King Louis XIV was known to enjoy hot chocolate, although he added egg yolk to his recipe to make it thicker.

Chocolate began to gain popularity, but its exposure was limited to physicians and the wealthy residents of France. Physicians used it to cure several ailments, including fevers, insomnia, fatigue and stomach problems. The wealthy could afford the high price and excessive tax on cacao beans, so it became a symbol of their high status in the community. It was often combined with milk, vanilla, sugar or ground nuts.

Chocolate And England

England discovered the joys of chocolate in the late seventeenth century. Unlike France, English residents believed that everyone should be able to enjoy chocolate if they had the means to buy it.

Chocolate houses were established to serve cups of hot chocolate to citizens. Politics were discussed around a cup of hot chocolate, tea or coffee, all of which were introduced to England within a few years of each other.

The Shape Of Chocolate

The history of chocolate was forever changed as chocolate eventually began to evolve into the treat that is popular today. Up until the early 1800's, chocolate was served in liquid form. At this time, Joseph Fry experimented with cocoa butter. When he replaced hot water with cocoa butter, it resulted in a piece of chocolate that retained its shape. Chocolate factories began to spring up all over Europe as people tried to discover the best way to serve the delicious treat.

Americans were introduced to chocolate during The Exposition in London, which was organized by Prince Albert. A few years later, Daniel Peter and Henri Nestle became a major part of the history of chocolate when they added condensed milk to their chocolate, resulting in the now famous milk chocolate bar. Confectioners started experimenting with both liquid and solid chocolate ingredients to create desserts that were unique and flavourful.

Chocolate And Controversy

Not everything about the history of chocolate is sweet. Churches have struggled with the question of whether chocolate should be allowed. Initially, it was approved due to its ability to alleviate many health issues. It was then deemed to be too indulgent, and some priests banned the consumption of chocolate.

For many years, Catholic Ecclesiastics tried to decide if chocolate was a liquid or a food because they needed to determine if it was allowed to be consumed during a time of fasting. When a group of Protestants crossed the ocean in North America, they banned chocolate because of their experience while living next door to a chocolate house in Amsterdam, calling chocolate "devil's food". Years later, the citizens of Amsterdam honoured the Pilgrims by naming a dark chocolate cake "Devil's Food Cake".

The history of chocolate is a rich and interesting one. While experts are not completely sure when the cacao tree was discovered or initially consumed by humans, they do know that its beans have been used for centuries for several purposes. Whether it was a part of religious ceremonies, a medical remedy or simply a delicious indulgence, chocolate has played a large role in many cultures. There are currently different types of chocolates, and they can be used for a variety of reasons. Chocolate has evolved over the centuries, but it remains a symbol of indulgence and happiness.

Chapter 2: Chocolate Information And Interesting Facts About Chocolate

Chocolate is a treasured dessert across the world, but few people realize how unique and special the decadent treat actually is. Knowledge of chocolate information and interesting facts about chocolate can increase a consumer's enjoyment of the sweets that they have come to love.

The Cacao Tree

In order to better understand chocolate information and interesting facts about chocolate, it helps to know how chocolate is grown and produced. Chocolate comes from the beans of the Theobroma cacao tree, whose name means "food of the gods". The cacao tree originally grew in Central and South America, but its popularity has led it to be cultivated in several places around the world.

Africa is now one of the leading producers of cacao beans, but the trees are also grown in the Caribbean and parts of Asia. The cacao tree is very fragile and has shallow roots. It grows best in rich soil that is located in a moderate yet humid environment. After five years, it begins to produce the pods that contain the cacao beans. While the tree may live to be one hundred years old, it will stop producing pods after the first twenty-five years. Each pod takes at least six months to become ripe, and it contains approximately forty beans within its fleshy pulp. The pulp alone is sweet to taste and is often used in drinks, but the seeds have a very bitter flavour.

The pods must be carefully harvested due to the fragile nature of the cacao tree. Workers use poles or machetes to knock the pods off of the tree before they gently cut into them to reveal the beans. The open pods and their contents are then placed inside wooden bins or pits dug in the ground. Banana leaves are placed over the pods to create heat that will prompt fermentation and reduce the bitterness of the beans.

The fermentation process helps define the flavour that the cacao beans will have once they are made into chocolate. Workers stir the pile to aerate it. After a day, yeast begins to grow on the pile, encouraging the breakdown of the bean and the pulp. The beans begin to blend together to create a rich, warm flavour. The length of the fermentation period varies depending on the type and quality of the cacao bean and can range anywhere from three days to a few weeks.

The fermented beans must then dry out substantially before they can be used to make chocolate. Drying is usually accomplished by spreading the beans out in the sunshine.

They must be rotated regularly in order to aerate the beans while preventing the build-up of mold. It usually takes one to two weeks for cacao beans to completely dry before they are sent to chocolate manufacturers.

Each package of beans must be thoroughly inspected before it can be used in the manufacturing process. They are first sorted according to size before they leave the cacao plantation. They must also be checked for any damage or pests before they are sent to the factories. These checks are done by sampling a portion of the beans and opening them for inspection.

A trained tester will also check the liquor, which results from grinding the beans. Every chocolate company has their own specifications for the size, quality and flavour of the beans they want to use, and all of these tests help them determine if that shipment of cacao beans will make delicious chocolate that meets their standards.

When consumers gather chocolate information and interesting facts about chocolate, they become more aware of how the food is produced. There have been investigations and concern regarding the working conditions on cacao tree plantations. Many chocolate manufacturers are now ensuring that their cacao beans comply with the Fair Trade Policy, and this has improved the conditions for workers on many plantations.

How Chocolate Is Made

One of the most fascinating aspects of chocolate information and interesting facts about chocolate is how it is made in a factory. Once the beans have been approved by the manufacturer, the true production of chocolate begins. The beans must be thoroughly roasted to accentuate their warm, chocolate flavour and deepen their natural colours.

The variations in heat, roasting time and moisture will be a large factor in how the chocolate tastes after production. For a stronger flavour, the beans must be roasted for a longer period of time, but the manufacturers must take care not to roast them for too long, which will result in a bitter flavour.

After roasting, the beans go through a winnowing machine. This cracks the shell of the beans while leaving the centre, or nib, intact. A fan then clears away all of the shell pieces before the nibs are sorted by size.

Grinding stones crush the nibs, and the heat from the process melts the cocoa butter, which is the fat in cacao beans, into chocolate liquor.

Cocoa butter and sugar are then added to the liquor along with several other ingredients before it is refined. This is the step in the manufacturing process that determines which type of chocolate will be made. Milk chocolate has a great deal of milk added to it, while dark chocolate does not contain any milk products. White chocolate will have more cocoa butter and sugar added to it, but it will not have any cocoa powder.

In the next step, which is called conching, the chocolate is kneaded as more cocoa butter is added to it. The final chocolate mixture is then tempered through cycles of heating, stirring and cooling in order to make the chocolate as smooth and pure as possible. It is finally ready to be placed into moulds to give it the shape that consumers are accustomed to seeing.

With the variety of flavours and types of chocolate available, chocolatiers and confectioners have been able to use their imaginations to create a diverse assortment of delightful treats. Chocolate can be combined with nuts, coconut shavings, cinnamon and fruit. It can be flavoured with a variety of seasonings including herbs and spices, and peppers are often coated with chocolate for a spicy yet sweet dessert. This ensures that people are sure to find a type of chocolate treat that suits their preferences, no matter how eclectic their tastes may be.

Interesting Information About Chocolate

One of the most interesting aspects of chocolate information and interesting facts about chocolate comes from the misconceptions surrounding chocolate. Its decadent nature has earned it a reputation for leading people into excessive indulgence. However, when consumed in moderate amounts, chocolate has several health benefits. It is also the source of several interesting facts.

The Aztecs thought that the cacao tree was sent from their god. They used it to cure ailments, improve overall health and as an aphrodisiac

Mayans used cacao beans as currency.

The Aztecs and Mayans both drank beverages made from cacao beans. The Mayans' drink was rather bitter, but the Aztecs learned to sweeten it with vanilla and honey.

Chocolate contains chemicals that release endorphins that reduce pain and increase feelings of joy.

Chocolate has nearly as many antioxidants as tea. Antioxidants prevent free radicals from damaging cells in the body.

Eat an ounce of baking chocolate to consume 10% of your daily recommended intake of iron.

Africa supplies nearly 70% of the world's cacao beans that are used to make chocolate.

Chocolate acts as a mild amphetamine due to the small amount of caffeine that it contains, so it boosts energy and increases alertness.

Napoleon always kept a stash of chocolate nearby in case he needed some extra energy.

Despite its high fat content, consuming chocolate does not raise blood cholesterol levels.

Similar to coffee beans, cacao beans vary in flavour according to the region in which they are grown.

Casanova mixed chocolate and champagne to create a unique aphrodisiac that he served to women.

America and Switzerland have some of the highest rates of chocolate consumption in the world. On average, a single American will consume more than 11 pounds of chocolate each year, while one person in Switzerland will consume over 22 pounds of chocolate.

Theobromine, which is extremely beneficial for humans, can be deadly for dogs.

Chocolate got its name from "xocolatl", the Aztec word for "bitter water" because of the drink they concocted from its bitter beans.

In the 1870's, Henri Nestle and Daniel Peter invented milk chocolate by adding condensed milk to chocolate.

The conching machine that is used to create smooth chocolate was invented by Rudolphe Lindt.

Chocolate may have properties that actually prevent tooth decay rather than causing it.

Nearly 400 cacao beans make up one pound of roasted cacao beans.

Chocolate does not contribute to acne breakouts or migraines.

Cocoa butter's melting point is slightly lower than body temperature which is why chocolate will melt in your hands and your mouth.

Its rich history has ensured that there is no shortage of chocolate information and interesting facts about chocolate. Beginning with the people of Mesoamerica, chocolate has had a reigning role in many cultural traditions. Whether it is used to symbolize wealth and importance or is given as an expression of love and admiration, chocolate has earned a status that many other types of food can never hope to reach.

Chapter 3: Types Of Chocolate

While many people will indulge in any chocolate that they can get their hands on, they may not realize that there are several different types of chocolate. All chocolate is derived from the cacao beans of the Theobroma cacao tree, but different preparation methods result in a variety of chocolates. All chocolate begins with the fermentation, drying and roasting of the cacao beans. They are then pressed to separate the cocoa butter from the chocolate liquor. The next step in the process determines which type of chocolate will be produced because it is this phase in which sugar, vanilla, cocoa butter, milk or other ingredients are added to the chocolate mixture.

White Chocolate

White chocolate offers a stark contrast from its darker chocolate cousins. While white chocolate is still made from cacao beans, the way it is manufactured allows it to have a unique flavor and appearance.
As with other types of chocolate, the cacao beans are fermented, dried and roasted. They are then pressed to separate the cocoa solids from the fatty components, known as cocoa butter. While other types of chocolate reunite the solids and the cocoa butter, white chocolate does not. Instead, milk, sugar and vanilla are added to the cocoa butter to create a creamy, white

treat. Then, just like other types of chocolate, white chocolate goes through the conching process to make it smooth before it is tempered.

Since it does not contain the powder or liquor of cacao beans, white chocolate has a very mild flavor. Some chocolatiers do not group it with other types of chocolate because it lacks cocoa powder and chocolate liquor. It does not have the health benefits offered by other chocolates because it lacks the antioxidants and nutrients that are found in the cocoa powder. However, white chocolate is the only type of chocolate that does not have caffeine. Caffeine is found in the chocolate solids, and since those are left out, white chocolate does not act as a stimulant.

White chocolate is frequently used as an alternative for those that are not fond of a strong chocolate flavor. Its mild characteristics make it perfect for nutty desserts, coating fruit or making drinks. In order for it to be labeled as white chocolate, it must have cocoa butter listed in the ingredients. If it does not, it is merely considered to be a confectioner's coating that is made of hydrogenated animal and vegetable fats. The confectioner's coating lacks the rich, creamy taste of white chocolate and has very little flavor.

Milk Chocolate

For centuries, chocolate was produced as an unsweetened liquid. In the early 1800's, chocolatiers began to find ways to make chocolate a solid treat. This strategy was improved upon in the mid-1800's by

Daniel Peter and Henry Nestle. They added condensed milk to their chocolate creations, which resulted in a creamy, sweet dessert that is now known as milk chocolate.

Milk chocolate is manufactured by adding sugar and condensed milk or milk solids to the chocolate liquor and cocoa powder before the conching process. Its flavor is milder and sweeter, and it has a much lighter color. Manufacturers must be careful to use milk products that will have a long shelf life so that the chocolate does not spoil before it is consumed. Since it contains more sugar and milk than chocolate, some chocolatiers and confectioners do not include it among the true types of chocolate. They prefer to use bitter or dark chocolates while adding their own milk products or sweeteners.

Milk chocolate is popular as solid bars, but it is also a favorite ingredient for hot chocolate drinks. While it is used in some recipes, milk chocolate can be difficult to cook with because it must be carefully tempered. It scorches easily, so it needs to be monitored when making fudge or other candies.

Bitter Chocolate

Bitter chocolate has the most natural flavor of the different types of chocolate, and it tastes similar to raw cacao beans. Once the beans have been pressed to remove the cocoa butter, the chocolate liquor is remixed with a small amount of cocoa butter. No sugars, spices or other ingredients are added, so bitter chocolate has a very raw chocolate taste.

Bitter chocolate is available as a powder or in a solid bar, and it is sometimes labeled as baking chocolate or cooking chocolate. It is also called unsweetened chocolate due to its lack of sugar. Many bakers prefer using bitter chocolate rather than dark chocolate in their creations because they can add sweeteners as needed, and the powder allows certain recipes to remain moist after baking. While bitter chocolate is ideal for cooking and baking, it is not meant to be eaten alone due to its lack of sugar or other sweeteners.

Most chocolate cakes, brownies or pies use bitter chocolate as their base ingredient and then sugar and other flavorings are added as needed. Bitter chocolate is also used for many types of fudge and chocolate candies and can even be combined with a variety of peppers and spices.

Dark Chocolate

Dark chocolate is one of the most popular types of chocolate. It is created by adding sugar and fat during the manufacturing process. Some types of dark chocolate may contain a trace amount of milk but most do not. Dark chocolate therefore has a richer chocolate flavor than milk chocolate.

Since it does not contain additives such as milk solids, it often has a chalky, dry texture. It can also leave a bitter aftertaste after it has been consumed, although this depends on how much sugar or vanilla has been added to the chocolate.

Several types of chocolate fall under the category of dark chocolate, including bittersweet, semisweet and sweet dark chocolate. Sweet dark chocolate, which may also be labeled as German chocolate, contains more sugar and only about 30% cocoa, while darker varieties may have as much as 80% cocoa. Bittersweet chocolate must contain at least 35% cocoa solids, but several brands may contain as much as 80% chocolate liquor.

Despite the vast difference in how much cocoa they contain, most dark chocolates are interchangeable in recipes. This gives bakers some flexibility and variety while using dark chocolate in their kitchens. Many confectioners use bittersweet chocolate in order to have the dark, rich flavor of chocolate with a little added sweetness.

Dark chocolate has gained in popularity over recent years due to studies that have illuminated its many health benefits. Its high cocoa content means that it offers several antioxidants that help fight off cancer-causing free radicals. People who eat dark chocolate also experience a sense of peace and joy because the chocolate triggers a release of endorphins.

Chocolate has been used for hundreds of years to cure many ailments, including headaches, stomach troubles and fatigue. Modern dark chocolate contains the same properties as the medicinal chocolate that physicians used in the past and therefore offers many of the same healing benefits.

Semisweet Chocolate

Semisweet chocolate is a type of dark chocolate that contains nearly half as much sugar as it does cocoa. The result is a very sweet, rich treat that can be used for various desserts. Semisweet chocolate is available in bars, powders, chips and chunks. It may also be shaved so that it can be used as a topping on cakes, ice cream or drinks. This chocolate is popular with amateur bakers because they like its additional sweetness.

There are no regulations about how much cocoa must be used in semisweet chocolate, so different manufacturers produce various intensities of chocolate flavors. Semisweet chocolate is generally considered to have a richer flavor than sweet dark chocolate, yet it is also sweeter than bittersweet chocolate. Semisweet chocolate is often used in baking, but it is sweet enough to consume on its own. It melts easily and is not as prone to scorching and overcooking as milk chocolate.

Semisweet chocolate chips are a common ingredient in cookies, and they can even be used to make a variety of candies, cakes, brownies, pies and frostings. Recipes that contain semisweet chocolate may not need as much sugar added to them due to the amount of sugar that was added during manufacturing, and many professional bakers avoid using it for fear of producing desserts that are overly sweet.

The many types of chocolate make it easy for bakers and chocolatiers to find the perfect chocolate to use in their creations. They can reach for a bar of unsweetened chocolate to use in cakes, or they can use white chocolate to satisfy customers that want a milder treat. While there are several manufacturers that produce the same types of chocolate, the flavors may vary depending on where the beans were grown and how they were prepared. The roasting process can alter the cacao bean's flavor, and manufacturers have perfected the amount of heat used and the time that the beans are roasted to meet their unique specifications.

There are even variations in the intensity of the flavor among each type of chocolate, giving bakers even more flexibility. Some manufacturers will even produce several types of chocolate to meet the demands of their consumers. Whether they want something bitter or super sweet, they can find a manufacturer that makes the perfect chocolate to suit their needs.

Chapter 4: Chocolate And Health - Health Effects Of Chocolate

Research has changed the way that people look at their favourite desserts. There have been many recent studies about chocolate and health effects of chocolate, and it looks as though consuming chocolate can provide many health benefits. When eaten in moderation, dark chocolate can have some of the same positive effects on the body as vegetables.

Which Chocolates Have Health Benefits?

There are many kinds of chocolate on the market, including dark chocolate, milk chocolate, bitter chocolate and white chocolate. The more cocoa that the chocolate contains, the more health benefits it has. White chocolate does not have a positive impact on health because it does not have any cocoa powder or chocolate liquor. Milk chocolate has more sugar and milk than actual cocoa, and those ingredients counteract any benefits from the cocoa. Dark chocolate, on the other hand, offers consumers a way to satisfy their sweet tooth while providing a variety of health benefits. According to studies that have tested the relationship between chocolate and health-health effects of chocolate, types of dark chocolate are treated much like a dark vegetable once they have been consumed.

Chocolate is derived from the Theobroma cacao tree. The theobromine in the cacao beans gives chocolate its bitter flavour, but it also has several health benefits. That is why types of chocolate that do not contain high amounts of cocoa powder or chocolate liquor are not beneficial. Dark chocolates, such as semisweet, bitter and bittersweet chocolate, have the highest amounts of cocoa in them and therefore have a positive impact on overall health.

In order to reap the health benefits of dark chocolate, be careful not to consume it with milk. Studies have shown that milk will counteract the positive effects of chocolate. Chocolate milk and recipes that combine chocolate and milk will not yield the same health results as eating dark chocolate on its own.

The History Of Chocolate And Health

There has been a link between chocolate and health- health effects of chocolate for centuries. Aztec and Mayan Indians would consume cacao beans to cure several ailments. Once chocolate was introduced to Europe, physicians would administer chocolate to patients for several health problems.
Chocolate was known to cure many issues, including fatigue and stomach pain. While chocolate is no longer prescribed by most doctors, there is a form of chocolate therapy that is becoming popular.

Julie Pech is a hypnotherapist who has devoted her studies to improving people's lives through the consumption of chocolate. She has studied the different ways that chocolate is used in modern culture and how it affects everyday living.

She can tell people about themselves by their choice of chocolate and how they dispose of the wrapper. Through her book and speaking engagements, Pech is revitalizing the belief that a simple bite of chocolate will alleviate several physical and emotional problems.

Antioxidants

Antioxidants are natural compounds found in many fruits and vegetables, and scientists believe that plants use antioxidants to protect themselves from environmental stress. Since chocolate comes from a plant, it also has antioxidants that benefit humans. The main antioxidants found in dark chocolate are called polyphenols, which fight contaminants from the environment. Polyphenols help prevent damage from free radicals that humans are exposed to on a daily basis, such as cigarette smoke and pollution. They may even help reduce the risk of heart disease because they prevent the build-up of plaque on the walls of arteries. Antioxidants also help to improve overall health by protecting the body from common illnesses.
A small amount of cocoa powder can provide as many antioxidants as several cups of green tea or even a cup of blueberries. The body recognizes the antioxidants from dark chocolate as quickly as thirty minutes after it has been consumed, but it is out of the blood system within six hours.

Heart Health

There is another large link between chocolate and health-health effects of chocolate. Dark chocolate has properties that can improve cardiovascular health. This is partly due to the many antioxidants that chocolate contains. When LDL cells, also known as bad cholesterol, begin to oxidize, they are able to stick to the walls of the arteries more easily. The antioxidants in chocolate, which are comparable to those found in red wine, prevent the LDL cells from oxidizing and building up in the arteries. Studies have shown that moderate consumption of dark chocolate reduces the amount of bad cholesterol and therefore reduces the risk of heart disease and stroke.

Dark chocolate also has properties that help to reduce blood pressure. High blood pressure has been linked to several illnesses, including diabetes, cancer and dementia. Patients who have eaten a small piece of dark chocolate on a daily basis have been found to have lower blood pressure than those who do not consume it.

Similar to aspirin, dark chocolate has the ability to thin blood. It prevents excessive clotting, which is often a key factor in the onset of a stroke or heart attack. While patients formerly took an aspirin a day to improve their heart health, they can now eat a small piece of dark chocolate. The polyphenols also help prevent against atherosclerosis because they prevent the clumping of blood platelets.

Energy

The Mayan and Aztec Indians gave warriors drinks made from cacao beans to gain energy and strength before battles. Dark chocolate can give a quick energy boost due to the amount of caffeine that it contains. A small taste of dark chocolate acts as a stimulant, and it increases alertness and improves brain function. Dark chocolate also has a high amount of iron, which the body uses to fight fatigue.

Mood

Dark chocolate contains properties that improve the mood of people who consume it. While it is still in the mouth, chocolate triggers the release of endorphins, which are hormones that increase feelings of joy and happiness. It also contains tryptophan, an element in serotonin, that causes the body to feel relaxed and at peace while acting as an extremely mild anti-depressant. Dark chocolate is even thought to work as an aphrodisiac because it makes women feel relaxed and happy.

Tooth Health

It was long believed that chocolate was a primary cause of tooth decay. Now, however, studies have shown that the opposite may be true. Unlike other sugary treats, chocolate does not stick to the surface of the teeth, so it does not have time to cause plaque build-up. Dark chocolate also has powerful antioxidants that may help prevent tooth decay.

Myths Surrounding Chocolate And Health

There have been many misconceptions regarding chocolate and the health effects of chocolate. One of these myths is that eating chocolate causes acne. It is not the chocolate itself that prompts skin breakouts, but the milk that may be included in the chocolate may irritate skin.

While milk chocolate may contribute to acne, dark chocolate alone will not. It is another common misconception that chocolate causes migraines. While this is a common tale, studies have not linked chocolate consumption to an increase in migraines. Many people also believe that chocolate is extremely high in caffeine and will therefore cause hyperactivity. Eating a large amount of sugary foods is more likely to blame for restlessness in children.

Beauty

The relationship between chocolate and health-health effects of chocolate is not limited to chocolate consumption. It can also be used in beauty products. The Mayans and Aztecs took note of how cacao beans seemed to moisturize skin while making it glow, and they often took baths with cacao beans and flowers.

The same properties that make dark chocolate an antioxidant powerhouse also allow it to be a useful tool for beautification. The antioxidants that improve cardiovascular health work in a similar manner on the skin.

They protect the skin's cells from the harmful effects of the environment, such as sun damage and pollution. This can give skin a more youthful appearance while keeping signs of aging at bay. The tryptophan in chocolate also prompts relaxation.

A chocolate mask is one way to benefit from the beautifying properties of chocolate. The chocolate will leave your skin feeling clean, refreshed and hydrated. To improve the mask's performance, allow your pores to open by sitting in a steamy room for a few minutes. Mix half a cup of cocoa powder with half a cup of honey.

Then add a sprinkle of oatmeal and a splash of cream to the mixture, taking care that you use amounts of each that will best suit your skin type. The mask should be creamy and thick. The honey will draw out impurities from the skin as it hydrates cells. The oatmeal will exfoliate dead cells for glowing skin, and the cream will act as a toner. Leave the mask on your face for fifteen to twenty minutes before rinsing off thoroughly.

Chocolate earned a bad reputation because of its high fat content, but recent studies have shown that it is not as bad as scientists originally thought. They have now determined that dark chocolate yields many health benefits as long as it is consumed in moderation. A small square of dark chocolate a day may keep the doctor away.

Chapter 5: Chocolate Recipe Variations

Chocolate is an extremely versatile ingredient. While most people think of it being used as a dessert, it can actually be used in a variety of dishes. Many chocolate recipes have been passed down through the ages, and each generation gets more creative with the chocolate dishes that they make. With the variety of chocolates available and improvements in technology, it has become easier to create chocolate recipes that are both delectable and memorable.

Chocolate Cake Recipes

Cakes are an easy-to-make addition for any meal or gathering. They are staples at birthday parties and weddings, but they can also be used as a simple finish to an evening meal. Chocolate cake recipes are abundant in cookbooks because they are very easy to make and they taste delicious. Most chocolate cakes use unsweetened chocolate, also known as bitter chocolate, rather than dark chocolate or milk chocolate. This prevents the cake from becoming too sweet, but it also helps to keep the cake from drying out while baking.

There are simple chocolate cake recipes, but there are also more complex recipes that may combine more than one type of chocolate. The cakes can be made even more delightful with the addition of chocolate frosting or fruit. With the variety of chocolate recipes for cakes that are available, it may even be difficult for everyone to choose only one favourite kind of cake.

Chocolate Candy Recipes

Confectioners have become very creative with the candies they can make from chocolate. While many people will eat semisweet chocolate by the handfuls without any additional ingredients, there are several types of chocolate recipes for candy available.

Fudges are extremely popular and are flexible enough to work with every type of chocolate. Dark fudge, milk chocolate fudge and white chocolate fudges have a rich full flavour as they melt in your mouth.

Pralines are a combination of nuts and chocolate and are the perfect blend of salty and sweet. Truffles can be made with a variety of ingredients to suit nearly every preference. Turtles, éclairs, and bonbons are just a few of the many chocolate candy recipes that are available.

The simplest chocolate recipes for candy are those for chocolate clusters or chocolate bark. There are also chocolate candy recipes that include items such as fruit or liquor that may form the centre of the candy or add additional flavours to the chocolate.

Chocolate Chip Cookie Recipes

Chocolate chip cookie recipes are easy to come by, but they are all very different. Some people like their cookies to be hard and crunchy. Other people like theirs soft and chewy, while some may prefer something in between. Fortunately, the variety of chocolate chip cookie recipes ensures that everyone will find a cookie that suits their tastes. Despite their name, chocolate chip cookies are not limited in their ingredients.

While most are centred on semisweet chocolate chips, they may also have a mixture of nuts or other candies mixed in. They may also have milk chocolate chips or white chocolate chips sprinkled throughout. Traditionally, the batter consists of an egg, sugar, butter and vanilla, but newer cookies are including chocolate or cocoa as part of the mixture. This results in a cookie that tastes almost like a brownie or a cake with a rich batter surrounding decadent chocolate chips.

Chocolate Covered Recipes

Chocolatiers are always coming up with new ways to use chocolate. One way that they do this is by experimenting with dipping items in chocolate. Almost anything can be covered in chocolate, such as potato chips, pretzels, nuts and even chili peppers. Even salty snacks are improved when dipped in delectable chocolate. Dip peanut butter, fruit or coffee beans in a pot of melted chocolate, or add some rich hot fudge to your ice cream to make it a sundae.

Some bakers will even coat their already decadent miniature cakes and candies in a hard shell of chocolate. The coating is usually made by combining melted chocolate and paraffin wax, which will help the chocolate form a protective shell.

Chocolate Desserts

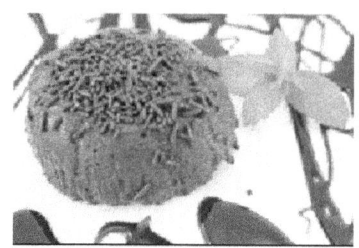

The sky is the limit when it comes to finding chocolate dessert recipes. Whether you need a simple sweet treat or an extravagant indulgence, a chocolate dessert is the perfect ending to a meal. The variety of chocolate recipes allows bakers to choose the ideal dessert to suit their needs.

Many children enjoy a small bowl of chocolate pudding or chocolate mousse after dinner. While chocolate covered strawberries may be the best way to top off a Sunday brunch, a tiered chocolate cake may be more suited to a wedding or party. Individual chocolate treats make great finger foods for business parties, or they can be arranged as centrepieces for an elegant affair. The vast selection of chocolate recipes ensures that everyone can find the perfect dessert for any occasion.

Chocolate Truffle Recipes

Chocolate truffles originated in France and are named after the rare mushroom in the area.

Chocolate truffles are made using a ganache centre, which is creamy. The centre is then rolled in a flavourful coating, such as confectioner's sugar or toasted coconut. There are numerous chocolate recipes for truffles because you can use almost any ingredient in them. Flavour the ganache with coffee or peppers. Roll the truffle in cocoa powder or ground peppercorns. When it comes to chocolate recipes for truffles, you can experiment with several of your favourite ingredients to find the perfect recipe to satisfy your tastes.

Chocolate Drink Recipes

With all of the chocolate treats available, we often forget about the drinkable versions of chocolate. Chocolate milk is a very simple yet flavourful way to enjoy chocolate. Hot chocolate is perfect for a cold day as you snuggle up with a blanket and a good book.

There are also chocolate drink recipes that are exclusively for adults, such as a white chocolate martini and other chocolate cocktails. Chocolate can even be mixed with coffee or soda to create unique, delicious beverages.

Chocolate Soufflé Recipes

A good chocolate soufflé is not as difficult to make as it would seem. In fact, it is an excellent introduction to soufflés for the baker that has never made them before. Most chocolate recipes for soufflés make a mixture that is similar to pudding that is flavoured with dark chocolate or cocoa powder. With the perfect amount of egg yolks, egg whites and air, the pudding will bake into a beautiful mountain of chocolate. Chocolate soufflé recipes may also include other flavours, such as coffee, vanilla, fruit liquors or a blend of chocolates.

Chocolate Covered Strawberries

Chocolate covered strawberries are a simple way to include dessert in your meal. They are elegant and refined, but they are also delicious and indulgent. They can be dipped in any kind of chocolate, although semisweet chocolate or bittersweet chocolate are the most popular choices. They can also be rolled in nuts or coconut before the chocolate hardens for a crunchy treat, and a swirl of contrasting white chocolate makes a beautiful addition to the dessert. You can even match the décor at your party by adding a layer of coloured sprinkles to the warm chocolate coating.

Diabetic Chocolate Recipes

People that have been diagnosed with diabetes do not have to sacrifice their love for chocolate. Fortunately, technology has allowed manufacturers to create sugar-free chocolates that allow diabetics to eat their fill without risking a spike in their blood sugar levels.

Alternative sweeteners are used as sugar substitutes and do not affect the original chocolate flavour. Every type of chocolate dessert or confection can be found in a form that does not have sugar. Cakes, pies, truffles, candies and drinks are all available in sugar-free varieties.

While some people may taste a slight difference in the sweeteners that are used, most people can satisfy their chocolate craving by using chocolate recipes designed for diabetics.

Lactose Free Chocolate Recipes

Since many chocolate recipes include milk products, it was difficult in the past for people who suffer from lactose intolerance to enjoy their favourite desserts. However, there has been a large portion of the population that is either allergic to dairy products or is unable to digest them, which prompted lactose free chocolate recipes to become increasingly available. There are recipes for egg-free cakes, muffins and cookies. There are even chocolate recipes for candies and drinks that do not include milk or eggs. Many lactose free chocolate recipes are also easy to adapt to gluten free or vegan diets, so everyone can enjoy their favourite chocolate dishes while taking care of their bodies.

There are many chocolate recipes available, so it is easy to find the perfect chocolate dessert for your needs. Special occasions may call for a more elegant or complex chocolate treat, but there are plenty of chocolate recipes for simple day to day indulgences. Easy recipes are available for bakers that are short on time or that are nervous about their first forays into working with chocolate. Whether you want a sweet drink that will satisfy your chocolate craving or a sweet and salty snack, a collection of chocolate recipes will help you be prepared for any time when chocolate is needed.

Chapter 6: Chocolate Cake Recipes

There are a variety of **chocolate cake recipes** that are rich and decadent. While most chocolate cakes call for unsweetened chocolate, there are others that use a variety of chocolates in order to produce a cake that is full of flavor.

Black Magic Cake

This is the perfect cake for times when you want a rich chocolate flavor with a moist texture.

Ingredients

1 3/4 cups all-purpose flour
2 cups white sugar
3/4 cup unsweetened cocoa powder
2 teaspoons baking soda
1 teaspoon baking powder
1 teaspoon salt
2 eggs
1 cup strong brewed coffee
1 cup buttermilk
1/2 cup vegetable oil
1 teaspoon vanilla extract

Directions

Combine dry ingredients in a large bowl, and use a spoon to make a well in the center.
Add wet ingredients and beat on medium speed for 2 minutes. The batter should be very thin and smooth.
Pour batter into 2 greased 9-inch pans or one 9X13 pan.
Bake at 350 degrees for 30 to 40 minutes. You will know that the cake is done when you insert a toothpick in the center and it is clean when you remove it.
Allow the cake to cool before you frost it.

German Sweet Chocolate Cake

This is one of many **chocolate cake recipes** that will quickly become a favorite in your household.

Ingredients

4 ounces of German sweet chocolate
1/2 cup water
2 cups all-purpose flour
1 teaspoon baking soda
1/4 teaspoon salt
1 cup butter, softened
2 cups white sugar
4 egg yolks
1 teaspoon vanilla extract
1 cup buttermilk
4 egg whites
12 fluid ounces evaporated milk
1 1/2 cups white sugar
3/4 cup butter
4 egg yolks
1 1/2 teaspoons vanilla extract
1 (8 ounce) package flaked coconut
1 1/2 cups chopped pecans

Directions

Grease a 9x13 pan or line it with wax paper.
Heat the chocolate in the microwave or in a double boiler, stirring frequently. The chocolate should be completely smooth and melted.

Combine flour, soda and salt in a medium bowl, and set it to the side.

Cream 1 cup of butter and 2 cups of sugar in a large bowl until it is light and airy.

Adding one yolk at a time, incorporate 4 egg yolks into the mixture and beat well after you add each yolk.

Add chocolate and vanilla. Alternate adding flour mixture and buttermilk and beat until smooth.

Beat egg whites in a separate bowl until they form soft peaks. Fold them into the batter, and pour the batter into the pan.

The cake should bake at 350 degrees for 30 minutes. Allow it to cool completely before applying frosting.

To make the frosting, stir 1 ½ cups of sugar, ¾ cup butter, 4 egg yolks and 1 ½ teaspoon vanilla in a saucepan. It should be allowed to cook on medium heat until it is thick and golden, approximately 12 minutes. Remove it from the burner, and stir in coconut and pecans. Allow it to cool before spreading it on the cake.

Black Forest Cake

This chocolate cake is layered with cherry filling for a sweet, delicious dessert.

Ingredients

1 cup milk
1 tablespoon vinegar
1 3/4 cups all-purpose flour
2 cups white sugar
3/4 cup unsweetened cocoa powder
1 teaspoon baking powder
2 teaspoons baking soda
1/2 teaspoon salt
2 eggs
1/2 cup vegetable oil
1 cup strong brewed coffee, cold
1 teaspoon vanilla extract
1 (21 ounce) can cherry pie filling
1/2 cup cherry liqueur

Directions

Grease two 8 inch round cake pans, and preheat the oven to 350 degrees.
Combine milk and vinegar to make sour milk, and set it to the side.
Sift together all of the dry ingredients and set aside. In a separate bowl, whisk together eggs, oil, coffee and vanilla. Gently stir in sour milk, and then gradually add the flour mixture, beating it only until is incorporated.

Pour batter into cake pans, and bake for 30 minutes. Allow the cakes to cool completely.

Mix cherry pie filling and liquor to make the filling. Allow it to chill in the refrigerator before adding it to the cake.

Mocha Layer Cake

This is a simple cake to prepare, but it will taste like it took hours. The several types of chocolate in the recipe give it deep, rich flavor.

Ingredients

1 (18.25 ounce) package chocolate cake mix
1 (3.9 ounce) package chocolate instant pudding
4 eggs
1 (8 ounce) container sour cream
1/2 cup cooking oil
1/2 cup Suisse mocha cafe
1/2 cup water
1 (8 ounce) package semisweet baking chocolate, divided
1/4 cup additional Suisse mocha cafe
2 cups thawed whipped topping
2 tablespoons butter
1 tablespoon light corn syrup
1 tablespoon water

Directions

Use a beater to combine cake mix, dry pudding mix, eggs, sour cream, oil, ½ cup instant flavored coffee and ½ cup water on low speed. Scrape the bowl frequently, and stop when the mixture is moist. Blend well on medium speed for two minutes. Stir in four chopped

chocolate squares and stir them into the batter. Pour the batter into two 9 inch greased round pans.
Bake at 350 degrees for 40 to 45 minutes.
Add the remaining amount of flavored coffee into the whipped cream. Layer the cakes with the whipped cream mixture in the middle. Heat the butter, corn syrup and remaining water and chocolate and stir. The chocolate should be completely melted. Spread the mixture over the top of the cake.

Extreme Chocolate Cake

This is one of the richest chocolate cake recipes you can find. The moist cake combined with the chocolate buttercream icing makes it superb.

Ingredients

2 cups white sugar
1 3/4 cups all-purpose flour
3/4 cup unsweetened cocoa powder
1 1/2 teaspoons baking soda
1 1/2 teaspoons baking powder
1 teaspoon salt
2 eggs
1 cup milk
1/2 cup vegetable oil
2 teaspoons vanilla extract
1 cup boiling water

Frosting
3/4 cup butter

1 1/2 cups unsweetened cocoa powder
5 1/3 cups confectioners' sugar
2/3 cup milk
1 teaspoon vanilla extract

Directions

Grease two 9 inch cake pans.
Combine all of the dry ingredients in a medium bowl. Add the remaining cake ingredients except for the water, and beat them with a mixer for about three minutes. Use a spoon to stir in boiling water. Pour the batter into the cake pans.
Bake at 350 degrees for 30 to 35 minutes. Allow cake to cool for 10 minutes before you take them out of the pans.

For the frosting, use a mixer to cream the butter. Add cocoa and confectioner's sugar alternately with milk and vanilla. Beat until it is thick yet spreadable.
Frost the top of each cake before stacking them on top of each other. Then frost the sides.

Chapter 7: Chocolate Candy Recipes

Chocolate candy recipes are abundant because the recipes are passed down over the generations. They are popular because they can be easily adapted to fit individual preferences, and little changes can make an already delicious treat even more delectable.

Kentucky Bourbon Balls

These easy –to-make little treats can pack quite a punch!

Ingredients

1 cup chopped nuts
5 tablespoons Kentucky bourbon
1/2 cup butter, softened
1 (16 ounce) package confectioners' sugar
18 ounces semisweet chocolate

Directions

Soak nuts in bourbon in a sealed container overnight.
Combine the butter and sugar before folding in the nuts. Roll into small balls and place in the refrigerator for at least 8 hours.
Melt chocolate in a double boiler, stirring frequently. Coat the balls with the chocolate and place on a tray that has been lined with wax paper. Keep bourbon balls chilled until it is time to serve.

Maple Walnut Fudge

This is the perfect fudge for someone that wants a chocolate treat made from white chocolate. Its consistency will melt in your mouth as you savor the rich flavors.

Ingredients

3 cups white chocolate chips
1 (14 ounce) can sweetened condensed milk
1/4 cup butter
1 teaspoon maple flavored extract
1 1/2 cups chopped walnuts

Directions

Melt the white chocolate, condensed milk and butter in a sauce pan or in a microwave-safe bowl. Stir frequently to prevent overheating and scorching.
Once the chocolate is melted, add the maple flavored extract and then stir in walnuts.
Pour the mixture in an 8x8 glass dish that has been lined with wax paper. Place the fudge in the refrigerator for at least one hour before lifting it out of the pan.

Caramel Clusters With Nuts

For the times when you can't decide if you want something sweet or salty, this is the recipe you should turn to. The assortment of nuts gives a crunchy texture to complement the smooth sweetness of the chocolate.

Ingredients

25 caramels
1 tablespoon butter
1 tablespoon milk
1 cup sliced almonds
1/2 cup salted peanuts
1/2 cup pecan halves
1/2 cup semisweet chocolate chips
2 teaspoons shortening

Directions

Place caramels, butter and milk in a saucepan over medium heat, stirring until the caramels have melted. Add the nuts and stir gently.
Drop the nutty caramel mixture by the spoonful on waxed paper.
Melt chocolate chips and shortening in a different saucepan, stirring continuously. Drizzle over the clusters. Allow the candies to set in the refrigerator.

Dark Chocolate Truffles

If you are looking for simple chocolate candy recipes to help you perfect your candy-making skills, this is one of the best. The easy directions lead to the creation of indulgent treats that will make your mouth water. You can also add spices and seasonings to make truffles that suit you perfectly.

Ingredients

1 cup heavy cream
2 tablespoons butter
4 (1 ounce) squares baking chocolate
2 3/4 cups semi-sweet chocolate chips

Directions

Combine all ingredients in a saucepan and cook over medium heat. Stir the mixture constantly until the chocolate is smooth and thick. Pour the mixture into a bowl and allow it to sit in the refrigerator for at least one hour.
Place small balls of the chocolate on sheets of wax paper. You can also roll them in powdered sugar, cocoa powder or toasted coconuts at this time. Store the truffles in the refrigerator until they completely harden.

Tiger Butter Candy

Tiger butter candy is a delicious mix of chocolate, peanut butter and cream. With those ingredients, it can't help but be delicious!

Ingredients

1 pound white confectioners' coating, cut into pieces
1/2 cup chunky peanut butter
1/2 cup semisweet chocolate chips
4 teaspoons half-and-half cream

Directions

Heat the confectioner's coating and peanut butter in a saucepan over medium heat until they are melted. Stir to mix them well.

Pour the mixture over a baking sheet covered with aluminum paper and spread into a thin layer. In another saucepan, heat chocolate chips and cream over high heat until the chips have softened. Stir until the mixture is smooth.

Pour the chocolate over the peanut butter layer, and swirl it with a knife.

Place the sheet in the freezer for 5 minutes. Break it into small pieces before serving.

Chapter 8: Chocolate Chip Cookie Recipes

Every baker has at least one chocolate chip cookie recipe that is his favorite, but more than likely he will have multiple recipes that he works from frequently. Chocolate chip cookies are a delightful way to indulge a sweet tooth, but they can also be served at formal occasions. Their versatility makes them an ideal dessert for all ages.

Triple Chocolate Chip Cookies

These cookies are for chocoholics that can't seem to get enough. The combination of semisweet chocolate chips, white chocolate chips and milk chocolate chips gives taste buds a chance to experience a variety of flavors.

Ingredients

1/2 cup unsalted butter
1/2 cup white sugar
1/4 cup packed light brown sugar
1 large egg
1/2 teaspoon vanilla extract
1 1/8 cups all-purpose flour
1/2 teaspoon salt
1/2 teaspoon baking soda
1/3 cup semi-sweet chocolate chips
1/3 cup white chocolate chips
1/3 cup milk chocolate chips

Directions

Prepare a baking sheet by lining it with parchment paper, and preheat the oven to 375 degrees.
Combine the butter and both sugars using a spatula. The mixture should become creamy after three minutes of stirring. Whisk in the egg and vanilla.
Combine the flour, salt and baking soda in a small bowl. Add the butter mixture and stir it until it is just

combined. Fold in the three types of chocolate chips. Use a spoon to scoop the mixture onto the baking sheet.

Bake at 375 degrees for 10 minutes. Allow to cool on a wire rack.

White Chocolate Chip Oatmeal Cookies

These cookies are perfect for those that want a mild chocolate flavor as they indulge in their favorite dessert. You can also add pecans or walnuts for an extra treat.

Ingredients

1 cup butter
1 cup light brown sugar
1 cup white sugar
2 eggs
2 teaspoons vanilla extract
3 cups all-purpose flour
1 teaspoon baking powder
1 teaspoon baking soda
1 teaspoon salt
1 1/2 cups rolled oats
2 cups white chocolate chips

Directions

Cream butter and both sugars until the mixture is smooth. Add egg and vanilla and stir gently. Sift the flour, baking powder, baking soda and salt, and slowly incorporate it into the butter mixture. Stir in the oats and white chocolate chips.

Drop the cookies onto a greased cookie sheet using a spoon. Bake at 350 degrees for at least 10 minutes. Allow to cool on wire racks.

Chocolate Pileup Cookies

This is one of many chocolate chip cookie recipes that will be a winner no matter where you go. The rich combinations of chocolate add to the already decadent treat, but the entire cookie becomes a masterpiece with the addition of coffee-flavored liquor and hazelnuts.

Ingredients

2 cups all-purpose flour
3/4 cup unsweetened cocoa powder
1 teaspoon baking soda
1 teaspoon salt
1 cup unsalted butter, at room temperature
3/4 cup white sugar
3/4 cup brown sugar
2 eggs
2 teaspoons vanilla extract
2 tablespoons coffee-flavored liquor
1 cup finely chopped toasted hazelnuts
1 cup semisweet chocolate chips
1 cup milk chocolate chips
1 cup white chocolate chips

Directions

Combine the flour, cocoa, baking soda and salt in a medium bowl.

In a separate bowl, cream the butter and both sugars. Add the eggs, vanilla and coffee liquor and beat thoroughly.

Gradually add the flour mixture until it has been well combined. Fold in all the chocolate chips and hazelnuts.

Use a spoon to drop the cookies onto the parchment paper. Bake cookies for 8 to 10 minutes. One minute after removing from the oven, transfer the cookies to a wire rack to cool.

Chocolate Mint Brownie Cookies

As if most chocolate chip cookie recipes weren't tasty enough, someone figured out how to make them even better. This cookie has a texture that resembles brownies, and the mint chocolate chips are a delightful surprise.

Ingredients

1 1/2 cups firmly packed light brown sugar
2/3 cup all-vegetable shortening
1 tablespoon water
1 teaspoon vanilla extract
1/2 teaspoon peppermint extract
2 large eggs, lightly beaten
1 1/2 cups all-purpose flour
1/2 teaspoon salt
1/3 cup unsweetened cocoa powder
1/4 teaspoon baking soda
2 cups mint chocolate chips

Directions

In a large bowl, beat brown sugar, shortening, water and both extracts until it thoroughly combined. Carefully mix in the eggs.

In a medium bowl, mix flour, salt, cocoa and baking soda. Add in shortening and beat slightly. Fold in the chocolate chips.

Use a spoon to drop the mixture onto ungreased baking sheets.

Bake at 375 degrees for 7 to 9 minutes. Allow to cool for 2 minutes before transferring the cookies to cooling racks.

Ideal Chocolate Chip Cookies

This is one recipe that is perfect for those that don't typically care for chocolate chip cookies. While it still meets all of the requirements to be classified as a chocolate chip cookie, it also has some extra ingredients that make it unique and amazing.

Ingredients

1/2 cup butter, softened
1/2 cup packed brown sugar
1/2 cup white sugar
1 egg
1 1/2 tablespoons brandy
1 1/2 cups unbleached all-purpose flour
1/2 teaspoon baking soda
3/4 cup semisweet chocolate chips
3/4 cup golden raisin and cherry dried fruit mix

Directions

Cream butter and sugars in a large bowl. Once they are smooth, beat in egg and brandy. Mix flour and baking soda before stirring into the sugar mixture. Fold in the chocolate and dried fruit.
Use a small spoon to drop dough onto an ungreased cookie sheet.
In a 375 degree oven, bake the cookies for 8 to 10 minutes. They are best served when they are still soft.

Chapter 9: Chocolate Covered Recipes

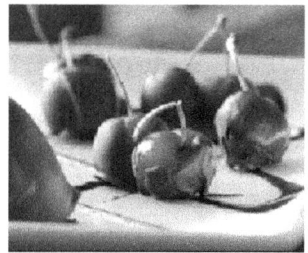

Some foods are wonderful on their own, but when you cover them in chocolate, they become amazing. One of the best ways to improve an already tasty treat is to coat it in chocolate. There are many **chocolate covered recipes** available, but you can make your own by taking your favorite food and dipping it in chocolate.

Chocolate Covered Graham Crackers

Many coffee houses offer expensive graham crackers that have been coated with chocolate. You can easily make your own that will taste just as decadent, and you can add finishing touches to make them look as though they were made in a candy shop.

Ingredients

24 graham crackers
2 (12 ounce) bags of dark chocolate chips

Directions

Use the microwave to melt chocolate in thirty second intervals. Avoid overcooking it so that it doesn't become scorched, but it should be thoroughly melted and smooth. Use tongs or dipping tools to dip the graham crackers in the chocolate. Set on a lined baking sheet to harden.

Chocolate Covered Potato Chips

If you thought that you couldn't have just one potato chip, wait until you sample this treat! The crunchy texture and saltiness of the chip contrasts perfectly with the smooth, sweet chocolate.

Ingredients

1 pound high quality milk chocolate, chopped
8 cups ridged potato chips

Directions

Use a double boiler to slowly heat the chocolate. Stir it occasionally until the chocolate melts completely. Use a candy thermometer or a meat thermometer to monitor the temperature of the chocolate.

Once it reaches 110 degrees, remove the chocolate from the heat and allow it to cool to 90 degrees, stirring continuously.

Dip potato chips into the chocolate using tongs. Once they are coated in chocolate, place the chips on wax paper to set.

White Chocolate Covered Pretzels

These are favorites with children. They love the contrast between the plain pretzel and the half that has been coated in chocolate. Let them have the option of rolling the covered pretzels in sprinkles or some other topping for an extra special treat.

Ingredients

6 (1 ounce) squares white chocolate
1 (15 ounce) package mini twist pretzels

Directions

Use a double boiler to melt white chocolate squares.
Dip half of the pretzel in the chocolate. Place it on wax paper.
Let set in the refrigerator for 15 minutes.

Chocolate Covered Cheesecake Bites

These little pieces of perfection are ideal for baby showers, weddings or other large gatherings. They are easy to prepare, but they will look like you purchased them from a confectioner.

Ingredients

1 cup graham cracker crumbs
1/4 cup finely chopped pecans
1/4 cup butter, melted
2 packages (8 ounces each) cream cheese, softened
1/2 cup sugar
1/4 cup sour cream
2 eggs, lightly beaten
1/2 teaspoon vanilla extract
24 ounces semisweet chocolate, chopped
3 tablespoons shortening

Directions

Place greased foil in a 9 inch square pan. Combine graham cracker crumbs, pecans and butter in a small bowl. Press the mixture into the baking pan.

Beat cream cheese, sugar and sour cream in a large bowl until the mixture is smooth. Add eggs and beat on low. Add vanilla and pour the mixture over the crust.

Bake the cheesecake for 35-40 minutes at 325 degrees. The center should be nearly set. Allow the cheesecake to cool before freezing it overnight.

In a microwave-safe bowl, melt chocolate and shortening and stir until it is completely cool.

Lift the edges of the foil to remove the cheesecake from the pan. Remove the foil and cut the cheesecake into small squares. Keep a few squares on hand to dip while the remaining pieces stay in the refrigerator.

Use a toothpick to help you dip each square in the melted chocolate. Let any extra chocolate drip back into the pan before placing the square on wax paper. Spoon a small amount of chocolate over each square to cover any inconsistencies. Allow the squares to sit for 20 minutes before serving.

Chocolate Covered Frozen Bananas

This is the perfect frozen treat for hot summer days. While it is very tasty, it also has several benefits. The bananas provide potassium, which is essential for good health, and the chocolate has several antioxidants. You will be satisfying your sweet tooth as you consume exactly what your body needs to stay healthy.

Ingredients

4 pop sticks
4 medium bananas, peeled
1 cup roasted peanuts, chopped
4 cups semisweet chocolate chips

Directions

Place a pop stick at the bottom of each banana so that it serves as a handle. Place it on a baking sheet that has been lined with parchment paper. Put the bananas in the freezer for one hour.
Use a double boiler to melt the chocolate until it is smooth. Place the chopped peanuts on a plate.
Coat each banana in the melted chocolate. The roll the chocolate coated banana in the peanuts before placing it back on the parchment paper. Freeze the bananas for another hour.

Chapter 10: Chocolate Desserts

If you are looking for a variety of chocolate desserts, you have an entire world of options to choose from. If you want something creamy and smooth, you can choose from chocolate puddings or soufflés.

If you want something crunchy, you can make your selection from a variety of chocolate covered treats. You can even opt for the healthier option of finishing your meal with some chocolate covered fruit.

Chocolate Mousse

This is one of the easiest and most scrumptious chocolate desserts that you can make. Its creamy texture makes it ideal for savoring each bite after a nice dinner.

Ingredients

8 ounces semisweet chocolate, coarsely chopped
1/2 cup water, divided
2 tablespoons butter
3 egg yolks
2 tablespoons sugar
1 1/4 cups whipping cream, whipped

Directions

Place the chocolate, butter and ¼ cup water in a double boiler, and heat it until it is all melted. Allow it to cool for 10 minutes.

Whisk egg yolks, sugar and remaining water in a small saucepan. Cook it over low heat, stirring constantly, until the temperature reaches 160 degrees, which should take about 1 to 2 minutes.

Remove the saucepan from the stove and whisk in the chocolate. Set the pan in ice and stir for about 5 to 10 minutes or until cooled. Gently stir in whipped cream, and spoon the dessert into small bowls.

Place the mousse in the refrigerator for at least 4 hours.

French Silk Chocolate Pie

This pie is one of those chocolate desserts that is considered sinful. Its rich flavor and creamy texture will make you close your eyes as you relish every bite.

Ingredients

1/2 cup butter, room temperature
3/4 cup white sugar
2 (1 ounce) squares unsweetened baking chocolate, melted and cooled
1 teaspoon vanilla extract
2 eggs
1 prepared 8 inch pastry shell, baked and cooled

Directions

In a large mixing bowl, cream butter. Gradually add sugar while beating with an electric mixer until the mixture is well blended.
Stir in the chocolate and vanilla. Add one egg at a time, but beat the mixture for five minutes in between each egg is added.
Spoon the mixture into the pie shell and refrigerate for at least 2 hours.

Chocolate Pudding

Chocolate pudding is one of the many chocolate desserts that you can throw together very quickly. If someone is joining you unexpectedly for dinner, whip up this delicious creation to serve after your meal. Add whipped cream, shaved chocolate or a strawberry to make it even more delectable.

Ingredients

1/2 cup white sugar
1/3 cup unsweetened cocoa powder
3 tablespoons cornstarch
2 cups milk
2 teaspoons vanilla extract

Directions

Whisk together sugar, cocoa and cornstarch. Add a little milk at a time to prevent dry lumps from forming. Heat the mixture in a saucepan or in the microwave until the mixture is shiny and thick. Add vanilla.
Chill in the refrigerator until serving time.

Dark Chocolate Cake

Dark chocolate cake is ideal for bridal showers, baby showers or birthday parties. This simple recipe will have everyone commenting on what a great baker you are.

Ingredients

2 cups boiling water
1 cup unsweetened cocoa powder
2 3/4 cups all-purpose flour
2 teaspoons baking soda
1/2 teaspoon baking powder
1/2 teaspoon salt
1 cup butter, softened
2 1/4 cups white sugar
4 eggs
1 1/2 teaspoons vanilla extract

Directions

Pour boiling water over cocoa in a medium bowl. Whisk them together until the mixture is smooth. Let it cool. Sift flour, soda, baking powder and salt in a separate bowl and set to the side.
Cream butter and sugar in a large bowl. Add the eggs one at a time as you beat them in. Stir in vanilla.
Alternately add flour mixture and cocoa mixture.
Pour the batter in three 9 inch round cake pans that have been greased.

Bake at 350 degrees for 25 to 30 minutes before allowing it to cool.

Chocolate Cheesecake

Cheesecake is synonymous with special occasions, but this chocolate cheesecake can be served at any time. Use it to welcome a new family to the neighborhood or as a delicious dessert one evening. You will love the creamy texture and rich flavor.

Ingredients

1/3 cup butter or margarine, melted
1 1/4 cups graham cracker crumbs
1/4 cup sugar
3 (8 ounce) packages cream cheese, softened
1 (14 ounce) can sweetened condensed milk
2 cups semi-sweet chocolate chips, melted
4 large eggs
2 teaspoons vanilla extract

Directions

Mix butter, graham cracker crumbs and sugar and press into the bottom of a pie pan.
Beat the cream cheese in a large mixing bowl. Add a little sweetened condensed milk at a time and beat until smooth. Mix in the remaining ingredients. Pour on top of the graham cracker mixture.
Bake at 300 degrees for 65 minutes. The center must be set before you can pull the cheesecake from the oven. Allow it to cool before placing it in the refrigerator to chill.

Chapter 11: Chocolate Drink Recipes

When most people think of chocolate, they picture a candy bar or a decadent cake. There are, however, ways to prepare chocolate for delicious drinks.
The first chocolate was consumed as a drink hundreds of years ago, and new ingredients have made the rich drinks even more enjoyable.

Thick Chocolate Shake

This classic is a wonderful way to cool off on a hot day. Add whipped cream and a cherry on top for a drink that is satisfying as well as easy to make.

Ingredients

2 cups vanilla ice cream
1/2 cup whole milk
1/4 cup powdered chocolate drink mix
1 teaspoon powdered egg whites

Directions

Blend all ingredients until smooth. Stir as needed to ensure that ingredients are evenly distributed.

Chocolate Martini

There is no better way to enjoy chocolate than to turn it into an adult beverage. A splash of alcohol will enrich the chocolate flavor, but it is still creamy enough to be considered a dessert.

Ingredients

1 (1.5 fluid ounce) jigger chocolate liqueur
1 (1.5 fluid ounce) jigger creme de cacao
1 tablespoon vodka
2 1/2 fluid ounces non-dairy vanilla-flavored creamer
2 teaspoons chocolate syrup

Directions

Combine all ingredients except for the chocolate syrup in a cocktail shaker with ice. Shake well until frost forms on the outside of the shaker. Chill a martini glass and dip it in the chocolate syrup. Serve the strained cocktail in the glass.

Chocolate Covered Cherry Shooters

This is another interesting way to enjoy chocolate. This alcoholic beverage tastes similar to chocolate covered cherries.

Ingredients

2 (1.5 fluid ounce) jiggers amaretto liqueur
1 teaspoon grenadine syrup
2 teaspoons chocolate syrup
2 teaspoons heavy cream

Directions

Pour ingredients over ice in a cocktail shaker. Shake well before straining into shot glasses.

Chilled Hot Chocolate

Hot chocolate is typically reserved for the winter months, but this drink allows you to enjoy it all year long. By adding some cold ingredients, you can have creamy chilled hot chocolate that is just as delicious as its winter counterpart.

Ingredients

1 1/2 cups warm water
4 (1 ounce) envelopes instant hot chocolate mix
2 cups vanilla ice cream
1 1/2 cups half-and-half cream

Directions

Combine water and cocoa mix in a blender and blend thoroughly. Add ice cream and half-and-half before processing until smooth. Serve in cold mugs.

Candy Cane Cocoa

This unusual chocolate drink recipe makes a wonderful gift during the holiday season. Its bright flavors bring feelings of friendship and warmth.

Ingredients

4 cups milk
3 (1 ounce) squares semisweet chocolate, chopped
4 peppermint candy canes, crushed
1 cup whipped cream
4 small peppermint candy canes

Directions

Scald milk in a saucepan. Add the chocolate and the crushed peppermint candies and whisk until smooth. Pour the drink into mugs and add small candy canes and whipped cream as garnishes.

Chapter 12: Chocolate Soufflé Recipes

Soufflés can be intimidating, but chocolate soufflés are well worth the effort. The airy texture and rich, warm flavors are rewarding enough to toss aside any doubts that you may have about your ability to make a chocolate soufflé.

Once you get started, you will realize that some recipes for soufflés are really very easy to follow and will result in delicious desserts.

Easy Chocolate Soufflé

This is one of the easiest **chocolate soufflé** recipes that you can find. The ingredients and directions make it fail-proof, and you will be able to enjoy a wonderful dessert that you can be proud of.

Ingredients

3 tablespoons all-purpose flour
3 tablespoons unsalted butter
½-1 teaspoon salt, to taste
1 1/2 cups milk
12 ounces bittersweet baking chocolate, coarsely chopped
1/2 cup brewed strong coffee
1 teaspoon vanilla extract
1/2 cup granulated sugar, divided
5 egg yolks
7 egg whites
Confectioner's sugar

Directions

Over medium heat, melt butter in a saucepan. Add flour, salt and milk and whisk. Cook the mixture until it comes to a boil and becomes thicker. This will be the sauce.

When you remove the sauce from the heat, stir in the chocolate until it is melted. Whisk in coffee, vanilla, and ¼ cup sugar until the mixture is smooth. Add egg yolks one at a time as you keep whisking. This will be the pudding. Let the pudding chill in the refrigerator.

Grease a soufflé dish with butter and evenly sprinkle a few tablespoons of granulated sugar across the bottom and sides.

In a clean bowl, beat the egg whites until they form soft peaks. Gradually add the remaining ¼ cup of sugar. Continue beating the mixture until it is soft and glossy.

Add ¼ of the egg white mixture to the pudding to make it lighter. Gently stir in the remaining egg whites.

Pour the pudding mixture into the soufflé dish, making sure that it is filled to the top. Bake at 375 degrees for 35-40 minutes. Sprinkle the top with confectioner's sugar.

Mexican Chocolate Soufflés

This is a nice alternative to traditional **chocolate soufflés**. The Mexican chocolate adds a unique flair to this yummy dessert.

Ingredients

4 (3.1-ounce) disks Mexican chocolate, coarsely
6 tablespoons (3/4 stick) <u>unsalted butter</u>, at room temperature
6 large egg yolks
6 large egg whites
1/4 cup sugar

Directions

Prepare 8 custard cups by buttering the bottoms and sides, and preheat the oven to 400 degrees.
Use a double boiler to melt the chocolate and butter. Once it is smooth, allow it to cool slightly.
Add 2 tablespoons of cooled chocolate to the egg yolks as you whisk them. Slowly continue to add the chocolate until the mixture is smooth. Beat egg whites with an electric mixer until they are frothy. Beat in sugar until the whites form stiff peaks. Fold the whites into the chocolate.
Fill the custard cups ¾ of the way full. Bake at 400 degrees for 16 to 18 minutes.

Chocolate Liquor Soufflés

The chocolate liquor gives these soufflés a slightly warmer flavor than using traditional chocolate.

Ingredients

1 tablespoon butter
white sugar for dusting
2 teaspoons unsweetened cocoa powder
2 tablespoons cornstarch
1/4 cup white sugar, divided
2 tablespoons butter
2 tablespoons bread flour
3/4 cup milk
4 egg yolks
4 egg whites
1/2 teaspoon vanilla extract
1/4 cup chocolate liqueur

Directions

Use the tablespoon of butter to grease four custard cups. Dust them with sugar.
Mix cocoa powder, cornstarch and one tablespoon of the sugar before setting it aside. Make a paste by mixing the butter and flour. Lightly beat one egg yolk in a bowl.
Bring milk to a boil in a heavy saucepan. Add the flour mixture and stir until it melts. Slowly pour the milk into the egg yolk, stirring constantly. Pour the mixture back

into the saucepan and let it simmer over low heat. Stir constantly.
It should take the custard about one minute to thicken. Remove it from the stove, and keep it smooth by stirring frequently. Mix the remaining egg yolks, vanilla, liquor and sugar mixture that you set aside. Stir in the custard, cover it with plastic, and set it to the side.

Beat the egg whites until they have quadrupled in size. Gradually stir in the rest of the sugar and beat it until the whites are stiff. Gradually fold in the egg whites.
Pour the batter into the custard cups. Bake at 400 degrees for 20 to 25 minutes. Serve hot with desired garnishes.

Dark Chocolate Soufflé

This dark chocolate soufflé will tempt your tastebuds every time you see it. The warm flavors of the Dutch processed cocoa will give you a completely new understanding of what chocolate can do.

Ingredients

1 tablespoon white sugar
1/2 cup Dutch Processed Cocoa
1/4 cup all-purpose flour
1/4 cup butter, softened
1 cup milk
1/2 cup white sugar
1 teaspoon vanilla extract
4 eggs, separated
2 tablespoons white sugar
6 scoops coffee ice cream

Directions

Grease a soufflé dish with butter and dust it with 1 tablespoon of sugar.
Mix cocoa and flour. Add butter and blend thoroughly. Scald milk before reducing heat. Add the cocoa mixture and whisk until it is smooth and has thickened. Remove the cocoa from the heat and add the vanilla and ½ cup sugar. Allow to cool. One at a time, beat in egg yolks. Allow the mixture to cool.
Whip the egg whites in a clean bowl until they become foamy. Slowly add 2 tablespoons of sugar and beat

until the egg whites form stiff peaks. Gradually add egg whites to chocolate pudding mixture. Pour batter into soufflé dish.

Bake at 350 degrees for 40 to 45 minutes.

Mini Chocolate Soufflés

These small treats are perfect for individual servings. The liquor adds a warm, dark flavor to an already rich dish.

Ingredients

Butter, for ramekins
1/2 cup sugar, plus extra to coat ramekins
4 eggs, separated
2 tablespoons Grand Marnier
6 ounces chocolate, melted
Confectioners' sugar, for dusting
1/2 cup chocolate sauce, for serving

Directions

Use butter to grease four small ramekins. Dust with sugar, but tap off any excess.
In a clean bowl, briskly beat ¼ cup sugar, yolks and liquor until it has been completely combined. Add melted chocolate.
In a separate bowl, beat egg whites so that they form soft peaks. Add remaining sugar and continue to beat the mixture until it becomes stuff. Add half of the egg whites to the pudding, and then gently stir the remaining egg whites. Pour it into the ramekins.
Bake at 400 degrees for 8 to 10 minutes.

Chapter 13: Chocolate Truffle Recipes

Chocolate truffles have been used for years as gifts as small personal indulgences. Quality chocolate truffles can be expensive, but don't let that keep you from enjoying them.

With a few simple recipes, you can enjoy chocolate truffles that are as delicious as ones that you buy in a candy store.

Easy Chocolate Truffles

This recipe is so easy to follow that you will find yourself wondering why you haven't tried it before.

Ingredients

8 ounces semi- or bittersweet chocolate, coarsely chopped
4 ounces unsweetened chocolate
8 tablespoons unsalted butter
1 (14 ounce) can sweetened condensed milk

Directions

Partially melt chocolates, butter and milk in a pan. Take it off the heat, and stir it until everything has melted completely. Add desired flavorings (fruit, coffee, etc.) until the mixture is smooth.

Pour the mixture into a bowl and allow it to sit for at least 2 hours.

Use a small spoon to mold the chocolate mixture into balls.

Fill a bowl with the coating of your choosing (confectioner's sugar, cocoa powder, etc.). Roll each truffle through the coating so that it is completely covered. Place it on parchment paper.

Serve at room temperature.

Luscious Chocolate Truffles

These little delights are packed with flavor. Use any coating of your choice to make them even better.

Ingredients

3 cups semi-sweet chocolate chips
1 (14 ounce) can sweetened condensed milk
1 tablespoon vanilla extract

Directions

Melt chocolate chips with sweetened condensed milk in a large saucepan. Stir to keep it smooth.
Remove the chocolate mixture from heat and add vanilla. Pour the mixture into a bowl. Allow to chill for a few hours to become firm.
Use your hands to roll the chocolate mixture into small balls. Coat them in an ingredient of your choosing.
Store in the refrigerator, but allow them to warm to room temperature before serving.

Chocolate Truffles

This is another easy recipe that can be adapted to fit your tastes.

Ingredients

8 ounces semisweet or bittersweet chocolate, cut into small pieces
1/2 cup heavy whipping cream
2 tablespoons unsalted butter

Directions

Bring cream and butter to a boil over medium heat. Pour the mixture over the chopped chocolate. Allow it to stand before stirring to make it smooth.
Add any liquor or flavoring.
Cover and allow to chill overnight.
Place ingredients for coatings on a plate. Scoop a small amount of the chocolate mixture and roll it through the coating. Place on parchment paper and place in the refrigerator. Allow truffles to warm to room temperature before serving.

White Chocolate Truffles

These truffles are perfect for those that don't want the slight bitter flavor that can come with dark chocolate desserts. They are still rich and creamy but have a milder flavor.

Ingredients

$1/3$ cup heavy cream, plus an additional 2 tablespoons
1 tablespoon unsalted butter
8 ounces good quality white chocolate, chopped into small pieces
1 cup flaked coconut

Directions

Bring heavy cream to a simmer in a saucepan. Add butter, and stir it until it has melted.
Add chocolate to the cream mixture and stir until it is completely smooth.
Remove the mixture from heat and pour it into a bowl. Cover it and allow it to chill in the refrigerator for at least 2 hours.
Roll the firm mixture into small balls. Place the coconut on a plate, and roll the truffles until they are completely coated.

Easy Chocolate Cookie Truffles

These chocolate truffles will be a hit with children. Serve them at your next birthday party or school gathering.

Ingredients

1 (16 ounce) package chocolate sandwich cookies, divided
1 (8 ounce) package cream cheese, softened
2 (8 ounce) packages semi-sweet baking chocolate, melted

Directions

Crush several of the cookies into fine crumbs using a rolling pin, and set them aside for later. Crush the remaining cookies and place them in a bowl. Mix the crumbs with cream cheese, and roll the mixture into small balls.

Dip the balls in melted chocolate and place them on wax paper. Roll them in remaining cookie crumbs. Allow to firm in the refrigerator for at least one hour.

Chapter 14: Chocolate Covered Strawberries

Nothing sparks love faster than food, and of course nothing sets off those fireworks faster than plump luscious strawberries drenched in chocolate.

A perfect treat for romance, but cute enough for a simple gift, these chocolate coated strawberries will be suited up for that special someone.

Divine Chocolate Coated Strawberries

These strawberries are perfect for parties. Set them on a colorful platter for a treat that all your guests will enjoy.

Ingredients

2 cups white baking chips
1 tablespoon shortening
18 large strawberries with leaves
1/2 cup semisweet chocolate chips
1 teaspoon shortening

Directions

Cover cookie sheet with waxed paper. Heat white baking chips and 1 tablespoon shortening in 2-quart saucepan over low heat, stirring constantly until chips are melted.
Rinse strawberries with cool water just before you are ready to use them, and pat dry with paper towels
For each strawberry, poke a fork or toothpick into stem end, and dip three-fourths of the way into the melted chips, leaving the top of the strawberry and leaves uncoated. Place on a wax paper-covered cookie sheet.
Heat semisweet chocolate chips and 1 teaspoon shortening in 1-quart saucepan over low heat, stirring constantly until chocolate chips are melted.
Drizzle the melted semisweet chocolate over the dipped strawberries, using a small spoon. Refrigerate uncovered about 30 minutes or until coating is set.

Chocolate Covered Strawberries

This recipe is the perfect one to use when you need a special treat in a hurry.

Ingredients

2 cups white baking chips
6 oz. chopped semisweet chocolate
3 oz. chopped white chocolate
1 pound strawberries with stems, washed and dried very well

Directions

Put the semisweet and white chocolates into 2 separate heatproof medium bowls. Fill 2 medium saucepans with a couple inches of water and bring to a simmer over medium heat. Turn off the heat; set the bowls of chocolate over the water to melt stirring constantly.
Once the chocolates are melted and smooth, remove from the heat. Line a cookie sheet with parchment or waxed paper. Holding the strawberry by the stem, dip the fruit into the dark chocolate, lift and twist slightly, letting any excess chocolate fall back into the bowl. Set strawberries on the parchment paper. Repeat with the rest of the strawberries.
Dip a fork in the white chocolate and drizzle the white chocolate over the dipped strawberries.

Set the strawberries aside until the chocolate sets, about 30 minutes.

Creamy Chocolate Covered Strawberries

The addition of orange liquor and heavy cream makes these strawberries positively sinful.

Ingredients

6 oz. sweet chocolate
3 tbsp. heavy cream
2 tsp. orange flavored liquor
1 tbsp. softened, unsalted butter
1 1/2 pt. fresh strawberries, with stems attached

Directions

Place sweet chocolate in the top of a double boiler and set over hot water while stirring to melt the chocolate. Add 2 tablespoons of the cream, the liquor, and the butter and heat the mixture, stirring until smooth.
Dip the strawberries in chocolate. Place on a wax paper lined dish and place in refrigerator until ready to serve.

Chocolate Covered Strawberries

The milk chocolate used for these chocolate covered strawberries makes them a scrumptious dessert.

Ingredients

16 oz. milk chocolate chips
2 tbsp. shortening
1 pound fresh strawberries with leaves

Directions

Insert toothpicks into the tops of the strawberries.
In a double boiler, melt the chocolate and shortening, stirring occasionally until smooth.
Holding them by the toothpicks, dip the strawberries into the chocolate mixture.
Turn the strawberries upside down and insert the toothpick into Styrofoam for the chocolate to cool.

Chocolate Dipped Strawberries

The piped chocolate makes these strawberries both delicious and beautiful.

Ingredients

24-30 fresh strawberries
6 oz. of white chocolate
8 oz. of dark chocolate

Directions

Wash and dry the strawberries, making sure the berries are fully dry as water will cause chocolate to seize up.
Melt the white chocolate in a double boiler or microwave.
Dip the strawberry in the white chocolate, holding onto the stem or "shoulders" of the strawberry. Give it a quick little twist and shake with your fingers to shake off the excess and then point it at the ceiling for a second or two to ensure that the chocolate adheres to the strawberry. Place on a piece of wax paper to let dry.
Melt the dark chocolate according to the instructions on the package. Dip the strawberry into the chocolate, making sure to let the excess drip off. Place on wax paper to dry.
Place some melted dark chocolate into a piping bag with a very small tip, or in a sealable bag with the little corner snipped off and drizzle or decorate the strawberries.

Allow to dry and cool, or place them in the freezer for 5 minutes.

Chapter 15: Diabetic Chocolate Recipes

People with diabetes often feel as though they must avoid every type of food that is enjoyable.
While they must carefully monitor what they eat, they do not need to shun chocolate desserts completely. There are many diabetic chocolate recipes available to help them satisfy their hunger for chocolate without damaging their bodies.

Chocolate Banana Mousse

This creamy treat combines chocolate and bananas in such a delicious way that you won't even miss the sugar.

Ingredients

1 1 oz. sq. unsweetened chocolate
1 cup evaporated skim milk
3 tbsp. granulated sugar replacement
2 egg yolks
1/4 tsp. salt
1 tsp. vanilla extract
2 bananas, sliced

Directions

In a double boiler, mix chocolate, ¼ cup milk and sugar substitute. Stir continuously until chocolate melts.
Pour a small amount of chocolate mixture over egg yolks and whisk thoroughly.
Pour the tempered eggs into the double broiler with the chocolate. Add salt and stir. Continue to cook and stir until the mixture thickens. Allow to cool.
Beat very cold milk until it is stiff. Fold the chocolate into the milk, and then fold in vanilla and banana slices. Place in containers in the freezer until the mousse is firm.

Chocolate Balls

These are easy to make and popular at parties. Take a plate of them to your next gathering or keep some in the refrigerator for a daily indulgence.

Ingredients

1/2 cup Margarine, room temp
2 tbsp. Sugar
1/3 cup Liquid sugar substitute
1 1/4 cup Flour
3 tbsp. Cocoa
1/2 tsp. Salt
1/4 cup Chopped nuts
2 tbsp. Raisins

Directions

Cream margarine and sugar until the mixture is light and fluffy.
Add vanilla and sugar and beat for 30 seconds at medium speed.
Blend flour, cocoa and salt before adding it to creamed mixture. Mix until blended.
Fold in nuts and raisins.
Use a small spoon to shape balls. Place them on a lined cookie sheet.
Bake for 20-25 minutes at 325 degrees. Allow to cool.

Sugar Free Chocolate Nut Clusters

These super-simple delights are ideal for satisfying the need for something salty and sweet.

Ingredients

5.6 ounces sugar-free chocolate
1 cup nuts, coarsely chopped

Directions

Place aluminum foil over a baking sheet.
Melt sugar-free chocolate in the microwave, taking care to stir occasionally to avoid scorching.
Add the nuts to the chocolate and stir until all nuts are coated.
Use a spoon to drop small amounts on the aluminum foil.
Allow to set in the refrigerator for 20 minutes.

Sugar Free Chocolate Butter Creams

These taste so rich and creamy that they seem as though they were just purchased at a candy store.

Ingredients
1 cup nonfat dry milk powder
1/3 cup cocoa
2 tablespoon paraffin wax
1/2 cup water
1 tablespoon shortening
1 tablespoon liquid sugar replacement (artificial sweetener)
3 ounce package cream cheese, softened
2 tablespoons milk
1 1/2 teaspoon vanilla extract
1 cup equivalent of sugar substitute

Directions

Blend milk powder, cocoa and was in a blender until it forms a powder.

Put powder in a double boiler and add water. Mix completely. Add shortening.

Cook over low heat and stir continuously until wax is melted.

When the sauce is creamy and thick, remove it from the heat. Add sugar replacement.

Allow to cool a little before dipping items in chocolate.

Beat cream cheese, milk and vanilla until the mixture is fluffy. Stir in sugar substitute.

Roll mixture into balls and allow to chill in the refrigerator. Coat each ball in chocolate before placing on a piece of wax paper.

Bittersweet Chocolate Sauce

When your fruit or yogurt needs a little extra help, drizzle this chocolate sauce over the top. It's the perfect way to add a bit of chocolate to any dessert.

Ingredients

3/4 cup skim milk
3/4 cup Dutch process or unsweetened cocoa
2 Tablespoons margarine
2 teaspoons vanilla
1 cup sugar substitute

Directions

Slowly add milk to cocoa in a small saucepan, stirring constantly. Allow it to simmer before stirring in vanilla. Allow to cool.
Stir in sugar substitute. Refrigerate the sauce until it is time to serve.

Chapter 16: Lactose Free Chocolate Recipes

More and more people are discovering that they cannot eat dairy products. Whether it is due to a milk allergy or because they are lactose intolerant, a large portion of the population is converting to a lactose free diet.

Fortunately, this doesn't mean that they have to quit eating delicious foods. There are several **lactose free chocolate recipes** that taste just as good as traditional desserts.

Chocolate With Chocolate Chip Pancakes

Serve these on a weekend morning, and your entire household will wake up happy.

Ingredients

2 ½ cups almond milk or other non-dairy milk alternative
2 T. apple cider vinegar
2 cups all-purpose flour
¼ cup pure cocoa powder
2 t. baking powder
1 t. baking soda
½ t. salt
1/3 cup packed dark brown sugar
2 large eggs, lightly beaten
1 T. dairy-free soy margarine, melted
3/4 cup dairy-free chocolate chips

Directions

Whisk together almond milk and cider vinegar. Allow the mixture to thicken for 5 minutes.
Sift flour, cocoa powder, baking powder, baking soda, salt and sugar in a medium bowl.
In a separate bowl, blend almond mixture, eggs and margarine until just combined. Stir in wet ingredients, but take care not to over mix.

Scoop a small amount of batter onto a hot griddle. When bubbles form around the outside edges, flip the pancakes until they are thoroughly cooked.

Dairy Free Chocolate Pudding

This pudding is so rich and creamy that you can't tell that it's dairy free.

Ingredients

3 tablespoons cornstarch
2 tablespoons water
1 1/2 cups soy milk
1/4 teaspoon vanilla extract
1/4 cup white sugar
1/4 cup unsweetened cocoa powder

Directions

Make a paste by combining cornstarch and water.

Cook soy milk, vanilla, sugar, cocoa and cornstarch mixture over medium heat. Allow it to cook until it boils and thickens, stirring constantly. Remove from heat and allow it to cool for 5 minutes. Refrigerate until serving.

Lactose Free Chocolate Cake

This is the perfect chocolate cake for anyone who suffers from milk or nut allergies.

Ingredients

1 1/2 cups all-purpose flour
1/2 teaspoon salt
1 cup white sugar
1/4 cup unsweetened cocoa powder
1 teaspoon baking soda
5 tablespoons vegetable oil
1 tablespoon white vinegar
1 teaspoon vanilla extract
1 cup cold water
1/2 cup semi-sweet chocolate chips

Directions

Mix flour, salt, sugar, cocoa powder and baking soda together in a large bowl. Add oil, vinegar and vanilla. When it is well combined, stir in cold water, and then add chocolate chips. Place the batter in a greased 8x8 pan.
Bake at 350 degrees for 30 to 35 minutes.

Dairy Free Chocolate Chip Cookies

These are a delightful way to enjoy chocolate without worrying about the lactose content. You can also substitute applesauce for the margarine for an even healthier treat.

Ingredients

1 cup of dairy-free margarine
1/2 cup of brown sugar
1/2 cup of cane sugar
1/4 cup of soy or rice milk
2 teaspoons of vanilla
2 1/4 cups of flour
1/2 teaspoon of salt
1 teaspoon of baking soda
12 ounces of dairy-free semisweet chocolate chips

Directions

Preheat oven to 350 degrees. Chop chocolate and set aside.
Combine margarine with both sugars until it is smooth and fluffy. Stir in milk and vanilla.
Combine all dry ingredients in a separate bowl. Blend them into the sugar mixture. Fold in chocolate.
Drop batter on cookie sheet. Bake cookies for 9 minutes or until they are golden brown.

Dairy Free Hot Chocolate

This is a great way to enjoy lactose free chocolate on a cold, dreary day.

Ingredients

1 cup water
4 ounces dairy-free dark chocolate
1/3 cup white organic sugar
3 cups plain unsweetened soymilk
½ t. vanilla

Directions

Whisk chocolate and water over low heat until chocolate is melted and smooth.
Stir in sugar until it has dissolved.
Increase to medium heat. Stir constantly until mixture is just about to boil. Then add soymilk and vanilla.
Cook until the drink is thick and smooth.

Part 2

Chocolate Cake Recipes

There are a variety of **chocolate cake recipes** that are rich and decadent. While most chocolate cakes call for unsweetened chocolate, there are others that use a variety of chocolates in order to produce a cake that is full of flavor.

Black Magic Cake

This is the perfect cake for times when you want a rich chocolate flavor with a moist texture.

Ingredients

220 g all-purpose flour
400 g white sugar
65 g unsweetened cocoa powder
9 g baking soda
5 g baking powder
6 g salt
2 eggs
235 ml strong brewed coffee
235 ml buttermilk
120 ml vegetable oil
5 ml vanilla extract

Directions

Combine dry ingredients in a large bowl, and use a spoon to make a well in the center.

Add wet ingredients and beat on medium speed for 2 minutes. The batter should be very thin and smooth.

Pour batter into 2 greased 22 centimeter pans or one 22x33 centimeter baking dish.

Bake at 180 degrees for 30 to 40 minutes. You will know that the cake is done when you insert a toothpick in the center and it is clean when you remove it. Allow the cake to cool before you frost it.

German Sweet Chocolate Cake

This is one of many **chocolate cake recipes** that will quickly become a favorite in your household.

Ingredients
112 g German sweet chocolate
120 ml water
250 g all-purpose flour
5 g baking soda
2 g salt
225 g butter, softened
400 g white sugar
4 egg yolks
5 ml vanilla extract
235 ml buttermilk
4 egg whites

Frosting
350 ml evaporated milk
300 g white sugar
170 g butter
4 egg yolks
8 ml vanilla extract
226 g flaked coconut
165 g chopped pecans

Directions
Grease a 22x33 centimeter pan or line it with wax paper.
Heat the chocolate in the microwave or in a double boiler, stirring frequently. The chocolate should be completely smooth and melted.

Combine flour, soda and salt in a medium bowl, and set it to the side.

Cream 225 g of butter and 400 g of sugar in a large bowl until it is light and airy. Adding one yolk at a time, incorporate 4 egg yolks into the mixture and beat well after you add each yolk. Add chocolate and vanilla. Alternate adding flour mixture and buttermilk and beat until smooth.

Beat egg whites in a separate bowl until they form soft peaks. Fold them into the batter, and pour the batter into the pan.

The cake should bake at 180 degrees C for 30 minutes. Allow it to cool completely before applying frosting.

To make the frosting, stir 300 g of sugar, 170 g butter, 4 egg yolks and 8 ml vanilla in a saucepan. It should be allowed to cook on medium heat until it is thick and golden, approximately 12 minutes. Remove it from the burner, and stir in coconut and pecans. Allow it to cool before spreading it on the cake.

Black Forest Cake

This chocolate cake is layered with cherry filling for a sweet, delicious dessert.

Ingredients
235 ml milk
15 ml vinegar
220 g all-purpose flour
400 g white sugar
65 g unsweetened cocoa powder
3 g baking powder
9 g baking soda
3 g salt
2 eggs
120 ml vegetable oil
235 ml strong brewed coffee, cold
5 ml vanilla extract

Filling
595 g cherry pie filling
120 ml cherry liqueur

Directions
Grease two 20 centimeter round cake pans, and preheat the oven to 180 degrees C.

Combine milk and vinegar to make sour milk, and set it to the side.

Sift together all of the dry ingredients and set aside. In a separate bowl, whisk together eggs, oil, coffee and vanilla. Gently stir in sour milk, and then gradually add the flour mixture, beating it only until is incorporated.

Pour batter into cake pans, and bake for 30 minutes. Allow the cakes to cool completely.

Mix cherry pie filling and liquor to make the filling. Allow it to chill in the refrigerator before adding it to the cake.

Mocha Layer Cake

This is a simple cake to prepare, but it will taste like it took hours. The several types of chocolate in the recipe give it deep, rich flavor.

Ingredients
517 g chocolate cake mix
109.2 g chocolate instant pudding
4 eggs
227 g sour cream
120 ml cooking oil
120 ml Suisse mocha cafe
120 ml water
227.2 g semisweet baking chocolate, divided
60 ml Suisse mocha cafe
135 g thawed whipped topping
30 g butter
15 ml light corn syrup
15 ml water

Directions
Use a beater to combine cake mix, dry pudding mix, eggs, sour cream, oil, 120 ml instant flavored coffee and 120 ml water on low speed. Scrape the bowl frequently, and stop when the mixture is moist. Blend well on medium speed for two minutes. Stir in four chopped chocolate squares and stir them into the batter. Pour the batter into two 22 centimeter round pans.
Bake at 180 degrees C for 40 to 45 minutes.

Add the remaining amount of flavored coffee into the whipped cream. Layer the cakes with the whipped cream mixture in the middle. Heat the butter, corn syrup and remaining water and chocolate and stir. The chocolate should be completely melted. Spread the mixture over the top of the cake.

Extreme Chocolate Cake

This is one of the richest chocolate cake recipes you can find. The moist cake combined with the chocolate buttercream icing makes it superb.

Ingredients
400 g white sugar
220 g all-purpose flour
65 g unsweetened cocoa powder
7 g baking soda
7 g baking powder
6 g salt
2 eggs
235 ml milk
120 ml vegetable oil
10 ml vanilla extract
235 ml boiling water

Frosting
170 g butter
130 g unsweetened cocoa powder
640 g confectioners' sugar
160 ml milk
5 ml vanilla extract

Directions
Grease two 22-centimeter cake pans.
Combine all of the dry ingredients in a medium bowl. Add the remaining cake ingredients except for the water, and beat them with a mixer for about three minutes. Use a spoon to stir in boiling water. Pour the batter into the cake pans.

Bake at 180 degrees C for 30 to 35 minutes. Allow cake to cool for 10 minutes before you take them out of the pans.

For the frosting, use a mixer to cream the butter. Add cocoa and confectioner's sugar alternately with milk and vanilla. Beat until it is thick yet spreadable.

Frost the top of each cake before stacking them on top of each other. Then frost the sides

Chocolate Candy Recipes

Chocolate candy recipes are abundant because the recipes are passed down over the generations. They are popular because they can be easily adapted to fit individual preferences, and little changes can make an already delicious treat even more delectable.

Kentucky Bourbon Balls

These easy –to-make little treats can pack quite a punch!

Ingredients

120 g chopped nuts
75 ml Kentucky bourbon
115 g butter, softened
448 g confectioners' sugar
505 g semisweet chocolate

Directions

Soak nuts in bourbon in a sealed container overnight.

Combine the butter and sugar before folding in the nuts. Roll into small balls and place in the refrigerator for at least 8 hours.

Melt chocolate in a double boiler, stirring frequently. Coat the balls with the chocolate and place on a tray that has been lined with wax paper. Keep bourbon balls chilled until it is time to serve.

Maple Walnut Fudge

This is the perfect fudge for someone that wants a chocolate treat made from white chocolate. Its consistency will melt in your mouth as you savor the rich flavors.

Ingredients

480 g white chocolate chips
1 (420 ml) can sweetened condensed milk
55 g butter
5 ml maple flavored extract
180 g broken walnuts

Directions

Melt the white chocolate, condensed milk and butter in a sauce pan or in a microwave-safe bowl. Stir frequently to prevent overheating and scorching.

Once the chocolate is melted, add the maple flavored extract and then stir in walnuts.

Pour the mixture in a 20x20 centimeter glass dish that has been lined with wax paper. Place the fudge in the refrigerator for at least one hour before lifting it out of the pan.

Caramel Clusters With Nuts

For the times when you can't decide if you want something sweet or salty, this is the recipe you should turn to. The assortment of nuts gives a crunchy texture to complement the smooth sweetness of the chocolate.

Ingredients
25 caramels
15 g butter
15 ml milk
95 g sliced almonds
75 g salted dry-roasted peanuts
55 g pecan halves
85 g semisweet chocolate chips
9 g shortening

Directions
Place caramels, butter and milk in a saucepan over medium heat, stirring until the caramels have melted. Add the nuts and stir gently.
Drop the nutty caramel mixture by the spoonful on waxed paper.
Melt chocolate chips and shortening in a different saucepan, stirring continuously. Drizzle over the clusters. Allow the candies to set in the refrigerator.

Dark Chocolate Truffles

If you are looking for simple **chocolate candy recipes** to help you perfect your candy-making skills, this is one of the best. The easy directions lead to the creation of indulgent treats that will make your mouth water. You can also add spices and seasonings to make truffles that suit you perfectly.

Ingredients
235 ml heavy cream
30 g butter
112 g baking chocolate
460 g semi-sweet chocolate chips

Directions
Combine all ingredients in a saucepan and cook over medium heat. Stir the mixture constantly until the chocolate is smooth and thick. Pour the mixture into a bowl and allow it to sit in the refrigerator for at least one hour.

Place small balls of the chocolate on sheets of wax paper. You can also roll them in powdered sugar, cocoa powder or toasted coconuts at this time. Store the truffles in the refrigerator until they completely harden.

Tiger Butter Candy

Tiger butter candy is a delicious mix of chocolate, peanut butter and cream. With those ingredients, it can't help but be delicious!

Ingredients
455 g white confectioners' coating, cut into pieces
130 g chunky peanut butter
85 g semisweet chocolate chips
20 ml half-and-half cream

Directions
Heat the confectioner's coating and peanut butter in a saucepan over medium heat until they are melted. Stir to mix them well.

Pour the mixture over a baking sheet covered with aluminum paper and spread into a thin layer. In another saucepan, heat chocolate chips and cream over high heat until the chips have softened. Stir until the mixture is smooth.

Pour the chocolate over the peanut butter layer, and swirl it with a knife.

Place the sheet in the freezer for 5 minutes. Break it into small pieces before serving.

Chocolate Chip Cookie Recipes

Every baker has at least one chocolate chip cookie recipe that is his favorite, but more than likely he will have multiple recipes that he works from frequently. Chocolate chip cookies are a delightful way to indulge a sweet tooth, but they can also be served at formal occasions. Their versatility makes them an ideal dessert for all ages.

Triple Chocolate Chip Cookies

These cookies are for chocoholics that can't seem to get enough. The combination of semisweet chocolate chips, white chocolate chips and milk chocolate chips gives taste buds a chance to experience a variety of flavors.

Ingredients
115 g unsalted butter
100 g white sugar
55 g packed light brown sugar
1 large egg
3 ml vanilla extract
140 g all-purpose flour
3 g salt
2 g baking soda
55 g semisweet chocolate chips
60 g white chocolate chips
55 g milk chocolate chips

Directions

Prepare a baking sheet by lining it with parchment paper, and preheat the oven to 190 degrees.

Combine the butter and both sugars using a spatula. The mixture should become creamy after three minutes of stirring. Whisk in the egg and vanilla.

Combine the flour, salt and baking soda in a small bowl. Add the butter mixture and stir it until it is just combined. Fold in the three types of chocolate chips. Use a spoon to scoop the mixture onto the baking sheet.

Bake at 190 degrees C for 10 minutes. Allow to cool on a wire rack.

White Chocolate Chip Oatmeal Cookies

These cookies are perfect for those that want a mild chocolate flavor as they indulge in their favorite dessert. You can also add pecans or walnuts for an extra treat.

Ingredients
225 g butter
220 g light brown sugar
200 g white sugar
2 eggs
10 ml vanilla extract
375 g all-purpose flour
5 g baking powder
5 g baking soda
6 g salt
120 g rolled oats
360 g white chocolate chips

Directions
Cream butter and both sugars until the mixture is smooth. Add egg and vanilla and stir gently. Sift the flour, baking powder, baking soda and salt, and slowly incorporate it into the butter mixture. Stir in the oats and white chocolate chips.

Drop the cookies onto a greased cookie sheet using a spoon. Bake at 190 degrees C for at least 10 minutes. Allow to cool on wire racks.

Chocolate Pileup Cookies

This is one of many **chocolate chip cookie recipes** that will be a winner no matter where you go. The rich combinations of chocolate add to the already decadent treat, but the entire cookie becomes a masterpiece with the addition of coffee-flavored liquor and hazelnuts.

Ingredients

250 g all-purpose flour
65 g unsweetened cocoa powder
5 g baking soda
6 g salt
225 g unsalted butter, at room temperature
150 g white sugar
110 g brown sugar
2 eggs
10 ml vanilla extract
30 ml coffee-flavored liqueur
115 g finely chopped toasted hazelnuts
255 g semisweet chocolate chips
170 g milk chocolate chips
180 g white chocolate chips

Directions

Combine the flour, cocoa, baking soda and salt in a medium bowl.

In a separate bowl, cream the butter and both sugars. Add the eggs, vanilla and coffee liquor and beat thoroughly.

Gradually add the flour mixture until it has been well combined. Fold in all the chocolate chips and hazelnuts.

Use a spoon to drop the cookies onto the parchment paper. Bake cookies for 8 to 10 minutes at 190 degrees C. One minute after removing from the oven, transfer the cookies to a wire rack to cool.

Chocolate Mint Brownie Cookies

As if most **chocolate chip cookie recipes** weren't tasty enough, someone figured out how to make them even better. This cookie has a texture that resembles brownies, and the mint chocolate chips are a delightful surprise.

Ingredients
330 g firmly packed light brown sugar
130 g all-vegetable shortening
15 ml water
5 ml vanilla extract
3 ml peppermint extract
2 large eggs, lightly beaten
185 g all-purpose flour
3 g salt
30 g unsweetened cocoa powder
1 g baking soda
335 g mint chocolate chips

Directions
In a large bowl, beat brown sugar, shortening, water and both extracts until it thoroughly combined. Carefully mix in the eggs.

In a medium bowl, mix flour, salt, cocoa and baking soda. Add in shortening and beat slightly. Fold in the chocolate chips.

Use a spoon to drop the mixture onto ungreased baking sheets.

Bake at 190 degrees C for 7 to 9 minutes. Allow to cool for 2 minutes before transferring the cookies to cooling racks.

Ideal Chocolate Chip Cookies

This is one recipe that is perfect for those that don't typically care for chocolate chip cookies. While it still meets all of the requirements to be classified as a chocolate chip cookie, it also has some extra ingredients that make it unique and amazing.

Ingredients
115 g butter, softened
110 g packed brown sugar
100 g white sugar
1 egg
20 ml brandy
190 g unbleached all-purpose flour
2 g baking soda
125 g semisweet chocolate chips
115 g golden raisin and cherry dried fruit mix

Directions
Cream butter and sugars in a large bowl. Once they are smooth, beat in egg and brandy. Mix flour and baking soda before stirring into the sugar mixture. Fold in the chocolate and dried fruit.

Use a small spoon to drop dough onto an ungreased cookie sheet.

In a 190 degree C oven, bake the cookies for 8 to 10 minutes. They are best served when they are still soft.

Chocolate Covered Recipes

Some foods are wonderful on their own, but when you cover them in chocolate, they become amazing. One of the best ways to improve an already tasty treat is to coat it in chocolate. There are many **chocolate covered recipes** available, but you can make your own by taking your favorite food and dipping it in chocolate.

Chocolate Covered Graham Crackers

Many coffee houses offer expensive graham crackers that have been coated with chocolate. You can easily make your own that will taste just as decadent, and you can add finishing touches to make them look as though they were made in a candy shop.

Ingredients
24 graham crackers
640 g chocolate chips
Directions
Use the microwave to melt chocolate in thirty second intervals. Avoid overcooking it so that it doesn't become scorched, but it should be thoroughly melted and smooth. Use tongs or dipping tools to dip the graham crackers in the chocolate. Set on a lined baking sheet to harden.

Chocolate Covered Potato Chips

If you thought that you couldn't have just one potato chip, wait until you sample this treat! The crunchy texture and saltiness of the chip contrasts perfectly with the smooth, sweet chocolate.

Ingredients

455 g high quality milk chocolate, chopped
600 g ridged potato chips

Directions

Use a double boiler to slowly heat the chocolate. Stir it occasionally until the chocolate melts completely. Use a candy thermometer or a meat thermometer to monitor the temperature of the chocolate.

Once it reaches 43 degrees C, remove the chocolate from the heat and allow it to cool to 90 degrees, stirring continuously. Dip potato chips into the chocolate using tongs. Once they are coated in chocolate, place the chips on wax paper to set.

White Chocolate Covered Pretzels

These are favorites with children. They love the contrast between the plain pretzel and the half that has been coated in chocolate. Let them have the option of rolling the covered pretzels in sprinkles or some other topping for an extra special treat.

Ingredients

168 g white chocolate

15 g mini twist pretzels

Directions

Use a double boiler to melt white chocolate squares.

Dip half of the pretzel in the chocolate. Place it on wax paper.

Let set in the refrigerator for 15 minutes.

Chocolate Covered Cheesecake Bites

These little pieces of perfection are ideal for baby showers, weddings or other large gatherings. They are easy to prepare, but they will look like you purchased them from a confectioner.

Ingredients
90 g graham cracker crumbs
30 g finely chopped pecans
57 g butter, melted
453 g cream cheese, softened
96 g sugar
30 g sour cream
2 eggs, lightly beaten
2.5 ml teaspoon vanilla extract
680 g semisweet chocolate, chopped
41 g shortening

Directions
Place greased foil in a 22 centimeter square pan. Combine graham cracker crumbs, pecans and butter in a small bowl. Press the mixture into the baking pan.

Beat cream cheese, sugar and sour cream in a large bowl until the mixture is smooth. Add eggs and beat on low. Add vanilla and pour the mixture over the crust.

Bake the cheesecake for 35-40 minutes at 165 degrees C. The center should be nearly set. Allow the cheesecake to cool before freezing it overnight.

In a microwave-safe bowl, melt chocolate and shortening and stir until it is completely cool.

Lift the edges of the foil to remove the cheesecake from the pan. Remove the foil and cut the cheesecake into small squares. Keep a few squares on hand to dip while the remaining pieces stay in the refrigerator.

Use a toothpick to help you dip each square in the melted chocolate. Let any extra chocolate drip back into the pan before placing the square on wax paper. Spoon a small amount of chocolate over each square to cover any inconsistencies. Allow the squares to sit for 20 minutes before serving.

Chocolate Covered Frozen Bananas

This is the perfect frozen treat for hot summer days. While it is very tasty, it also has several benefits. The bananas provide potassium, which is essential for good health, and the chocolate has several antioxidants. You will be satisfying your sweet tooth as you consume exactly what your body needs to stay healthy.

Ingredients
4 pop sticks
4 medium bananas, peeled
161 g roasted peanuts, chopped
719 semisweet chocolate chips

Directions
Place a pop stick at the bottom of each banana so that it serves as a handle. Place it on a baking sheet that has been lined with parchment paper. Put the bananas in the freezer for one hour.

Use a double boiler to melt the chocolate until it is smooth. Place the chopped peanuts on a plate.

Coat each banana in the melted chocolate. The roll the chocolate coated banana in the peanuts before placing it back on the parchment paper. Freeze the bananas for another hour.

Chocolate Desserts

If you are looking for a variety of chocolate desserts, you have an entire world of options to choose from. If you want something creamy and smooth, you can choose from chocolate puddings or soufflés. If you want something crunchy, you can make your selection from a variety of chocolate covered treats. You can even opt for the healthier option of finishing your meal with some chocolate covered fruit.

Chocolate Mousse

This is one of the easiest and most scrumptious **chocolate desserts** that you can make. Its creamy texture makes it ideal for savoring each bite after a nice dinner.

Ingredients
224 g semisweet chocolate, coarsely chopped
120 ml water, divided
30 g butter
3 egg yolks
25 g sugar
295 ml whipping cream, whipped

Directions
Place the chocolate, butter and 59 ml water in a double boiler, and heat it until it is all melted. Allow it to cool for 10 minutes.

Whisk egg yolks, sugar and remaining water in a small saucepan. Cook it over low heat, stirring constantly, until the temperature reaches 71 degrees C, which should take about 1 to 2 minutes.

Remove the saucepan from the stove and whisk in the chocolate. Set the pan in ice and stir for about 5 to 10 minutes or until cooled. Gently stir in whipped cream, and spoon the dessert into small bowls.

Place the mousse in the refrigerator for at least 4 hours.

French Silk Chocolate Pie

This pie is one of those **chocolate desserts** that is considered sinful. Its rich flavor and creamy texture will make you close your eyes as you relish every bite.

Ingredients
115 g butter, room temperature
150 g white sugar
56 g unsweetened baking chocolate, melted and cooled
5 ml vanilla extract
2 eggs
1 prepared 20 centimeter pastry shell, baked and cooled

Directions
In a large mixing bowl, cream butter. Gradually add sugar while beating with an electric mixer until the mixture is well blended.

Stir in the chocolate and vanilla. Add one egg at a time, but beat the mixture for five minutes in between each egg is added.

Spoon the mixture into the pie shell and refrigerate for at least 2 hours.

Chocolate Pudding

Chocolate pudding is one of the many chocolate desserts that you can throw together very quickly. If someone is joining you unexpectedly for dinner, whip up this delicious creation to serve after your meal. Add whipped cream, shaved chocolate or a strawberry to make it even more delectable.

Ingredients
100 g white sugar
30 g unsweetened cocoa powder
25 g cornstarch
475 ml milk
10 ml vanilla extract

Directions
Whisk together sugar, cocoa and cornstarch. Add a little milk at a time to prevent dry lumps from forming.
Heat the mixture in a saucepan or in the microwave until the mixture is shiny and thick. Add vanilla.
Chill in the refrigerator until serving time.

Dark Chocolate Cake

Dark chocolate cake is ideal for bridal showers, baby showers or birthday parties. This simple recipe will have everyone commenting on what a great baker you are.

Ingredients
475 ml boiling water
85 g unsweetened cocoa powder
345 g all-purpose flour
9 g baking soda
2 g baking powder
3 g salt
225 g butter, softened
450 g white sugar
4 eggs
8 ml vanilla extract

Directions
Pour boiling water over cocoa in a medium bowl. Whisk them together until the mixture is smooth. Let it cool. Sift flour, soda, baking powder and salt in a separate bowl and set to the side.
Cream butter and sugar in a large bowl. Add the eggs one at a time as you beat them in. Stir in vanilla.
Alternately add flour mixture and cocoa mixture.
Pour the batter in three 22 centimeters round cake pans that have been greased.
Bake at 180 degrees C for 25 to 30 minutes before allowing it to cool.

Chocolate Cheesecake

Cheesecake is synonymous with special occasions, but this chocolate cheesecake can be served at any time. Use it to welcome a new family to the neighborhood or as a delicious dessert one evening. You will love the creamy texture and rich flavor.

Ingredients
75 g butter or margarine, melted
105 g graham cracker crumbs
50 g sugar
672 g cream cheese, softened
414 ml sweetened condensed milk
335 g semi-sweet chocolate chips, melted
4 large eggs
10 ml vanilla extract

Directions
Mix butter, graham cracker crumbs and sugar and press into the bottom of a pie pan.

Beat the cream cheese in a large mixing bowl. Add a little sweetened condensed milk at a time and beat until smooth. Mix in the remaining ingredients. Pour on top of the graham cracker mixture.

Bake at 150 degrees C for 65 minutes. The center must be set before you can pull the cheesecake from the oven. Allow it to cool before placing it in the refrigerator to chill.

Chocolate Drink Recipes

When most people think of chocolate, they picture a candy bar or a decadent cake. There are, however, ways to prepare chocolate for delicious drinks. The first chocolate was consumed as a drink hundreds of years ago, and new ingredients have made the rich drinks even more enjoyable.

Thick Chocolate Shake

This classic is a wonderful way to cool off on a hot day. Add whipped cream and a cherry on top for a drink that is satisfying as well as easy to make.
Ingredients

265 g vanilla ice cream
120 ml whole milk
20 g powdered chocolate drink mix
2 g powdered egg whites
Directions
Blend all ingredients until smooth. Stir as needed to ensure that ingredients are evenly distributed.

Chocolate Martini

There is no better way to enjoy chocolate than to turn it into an adult beverage. A splash of alcohol will enrich the chocolate flavor, but it is still creamy enough to be considered a dessert.

Ingredients

45 ml chocolate liqueur
45 ml creme de cacao
15 ml vodka
70 ml non-dairy vanilla-flavored creamer
10 ml chocolate syrup

Directions

Combine all ingredients except for the chocolate syrup in a cocktail shaker with ice. Shake well until frost forms on the outside of the shaker. Chill a martini glass and dip it in the chocolate syrup. Serve the strained cocktail in the glass.

Chocolate Covered Cherry Shooters

This is another interesting way to enjoy chocolate. This alcoholic beverage tastes similar to chocolate covered cherries.

Ingredients

90 ml amaretto liqueur
5 ml grenadine syrup
10 ml chocolate syrup
10 ml heavy cream

Directions

Pour ingredients over ice in a cocktail shaker. Shake well before straining into shot glasses.

Chilled Hot Chocolate

Hot chocolate is typically reserved for the winter months, but this drink allows you to enjoy it all year long. By adding some cold ingredients, you can have creamy chilled hot chocolate that is just as delicious as its winter counterpart.

Ingredients
355 ml warm water
112 g instant hot chocolate mix
265 g vanilla ice cream
355 ml half-and-half cream

Directions
Combine water and cocoa mix in a blender and blend thoroughly. Add ice cream and half-and-half before processing until smooth. Serve in cold mugs.

Candy Cane Cocoa

This unusual chocolate drink recipe makes a wonderful gift during the holiday season. Its bright flavors bring feelings of friendship and warmth.

Ingredients

950 ml milk
84 g semisweet chocolate, chopped
4 peppermint candy canes, crushed
60 g whipped cream
4 small peppermint candy canes

Directions

Scald milk in a saucepan. Add the chocolate and the crushed peppermint candies and whisk until smooth. Pour the drink into mugs and add small candy canes and whipped cream as garnishes.

Chocolate Souffle Recipes

Soufflés can be intimidating, but chocolate soufflés are well worth the effort. The airy texture and rich, warm flavors are rewarding enough to toss aside any doubts that you may have about your ability to make a **chocolate soufflé**. Once you get started, you will realize that some recipes for soufflés are really very easy to follow and will result in delicious desserts.

Easy Chocolate Soufflé

This is one of the easiest **chocolate soufflé** recipes that you can find. The ingredients and directions make it fail-proof, and you will be able to enjoy a wonderful dessert that you can be proud of.
Ingredients

18 g all-purpose flour
43 g unsalted butter
Salt to taste
354 ml milk
340 g bittersweet baking chocolate, coarsely chopped
118 ml brewed strong coffee
5 ml vanilla extract
96 g granulated sugar, divided
5 egg yolks
7 egg whites
Confectioner's sugar

Directions

Over medium heat, melt butter in a saucepan. Add flour, salt and milk and whisk. Cook the mixture until it comes to a boil and becomes thicker. This will be the sauce.

When you remove the sauce from the heat, stir in the chocolate until it is melted. Whisk in coffee, vanilla, and 48 g sugar until the mixture is smooth. Add egg yolks one at a time as you keep whisking. This will be the pudding. Let the pudding chill in the refrigerator.

Grease a soufflé dish with butter and evenly sprinkle a few tablespoons of granulated sugar across the bottom and sides.

In a clean bowl, beat the egg whites until they form soft peaks. Gradually add the remaining 48 g of sugar. Continue beating the mixture until it is soft and glossy.

Add ¼ of the egg white mixture to the pudding to make it lighter. Gently stir in the remaining egg whites.

Pour the pudding mixture into the soufflé dish, making sure that it is filled to the top.

Bake at 190 degrees C for 35-40 minutes. Sprinkle the top with confectioner's sugar.

Mexican Chocolate Soufflés

This is a nice alternative to traditional **chocolate soufflés**. The Mexican chocolate adds a unique flair to this yummy dessert.

Ingredients
351 g Mexican chocolate, coarsely
86 g unsalted butter, at room temperature
6 large egg yolks
6 large egg whites
48 g sugar

Directions
Prepare 8 custard cups by buttering the bottoms and sides, and preheat the oven to 200 degrees C.
Use a double boiler to melt the chocolate and butter. Once it is smooth, allow it to cool slightly.
Add 30 g of cooled chocolate to the egg yolks as you whisk them. Slowly continue to add the chocolate until the mixture is smooth. Beat egg whites with an electric mixer until they are frothy. Beat in sugar until the whites form stiff peaks. Fold the whites into the chocolate.
Fill the custard cups ¾ of the way full. Bake at 200 degrees C for 16 to 18 minutes.

Chocolate Liquor Soufflés

The chocolate liquor gives these soufflés a slightly warmer flavor than using traditional chocolate.

Ingredients

15 g butter, for ramekins
White sugar for dusting
4 g unsweetened cocoa powder
15 g cornstarch
50 g white sugar, divided
30 g butter
15 g bread flour
180 ml milk
4 egg yolks
4 egg whites
3 ml vanilla extract
60 ml chocolate liquor

Directions

Use the tablespoon of butter to grease four custard cups. Dust them with sugar.

Mix cocoa powder, cornstarch and one tablespoon of the sugar before setting it aside. Make a paste by mixing the butter and flour. Lightly beat one egg yolk in a bowl.

Bring milk to a boil in a heavy saucepan. Add the flour mixture and stir until it melts. Slowly pour the milk into the egg yolk, stirring constantly. Pour the mixture back into the saucepan and let it simmer over low heat. Stir constantly.

It should take the custard about one minute to thicken. Remove it from the stove, and keep it smooth by stirring frequently. Mix the remaining egg yolks, vanilla, liquor and sugar mixture that you set aside. Stir in the custard, cover it with plastic, and set it to the side.
Beat the egg whites until they have quadrupled in size. Gradually stir in the rest of the sugar and beat it until the whites are stiff. Gradually fold in the egg whites.

Pour the batter into the custard cups. Bake at 200 degrees C for 20 to 25 minutes. Serve hot with desired garnishes.

Dark Chocolate Soufflé

This dark chocolate soufflé will tempt your taste buds every time you see it. The warm flavors of the Dutch processed cocoa will give you a completely new understanding of what chocolate can do.

Ingredients
10 g white sugar
45 g Dutch Processed Cocoa
30 g all-purpose flour
55 g butter, softened
235 ml milk
100 g white sugar
5 ml vanilla extract
4 eggs, separated
25 g white sugar

Directions
Grease a soufflé dish with butter and dust it with 10 g of sugar.

Mix cocoa and flour. Add butter and blend thoroughly. Scald milk before reducing heat. Add the cocoa mixture and whisk until it is smooth and has thickened. Remove the cocoa from the heat and add the vanilla and 100 g sugar. Allow to cool. One at a time, beat in egg yolks. Allow the mixture to cool.

Whip the egg whites in a clean bowl until they become foamy. Slowly add 25 g of sugar and beat until the egg whites form stiff peaks. Gradually add egg whites to chocolate pudding mixture. Pour batter into soufflé dish.

Bake at 180 C degrees for 40 to 45 minutes.

Mini Chocolate Soufflés

These small treats are perfect for individual servings. The liquor adds a warm, dark flavor to an already rich dish.

Ingredients

Butter, for ramekins
65 g sugar, plus extra to coat ramekins
4 eggs, separated
30 ml Grand Marnier
170 g chocolate, melted
Confectioners' sugar, for dusting
118 ml chocolate sauce, for serving

Directions

Use butter to grease four small ramekins. Dust with sugar, but tap off any excess.

In a clean bowl, briskly beat 48 g sugar, yolks and liquor until it has been completely combined. Add melted chocolate.

In a separate bowl, beat egg whites so that they form soft peaks. Add remaining sugar and continue to beat the mixture until it becomes stuff. Add half of the egg whites to the pudding, and then gently stir the remaining egg whites. Pour it into the ramekins.

Bake at 200 degrees C for 8 to 10 minutes.

Chocolate Truffle Recipes

Chocolate truffles have been used for years as gifts as small personal indulgences. Quality chocolate truffles can be expensive, but don't let that keep you from enjoying them. With a few simple recipes, you can enjoy chocolate truffles that are as delicious as ones that you buy in a candy store.

Easy Chocolate Truffles

This recipe is so easy to follow that you will find yourself wondering why you haven't tried it before.

Ingredients

225 g good-quality semisweet chocolate, coarsely chopped
110 g unsweetened chocolate
115 g unsalted butter
385 ml sweetened condensed milk

Directions

Partially melt chocolates, butter and milk in a pan. Take it off the heat, and stir it until everything has melted completely. Add desired flavorings (fruit, coffee, etc.) until the mixture is smooth.

Pour the mixture into a bowl and allow it to sit for at least 2 hours.

Use a small spoon to mold the chocolate mixture into balls.

Fill a bowl with the coating of your choosing (confectioner's sugar, cocoa powder, etc.). Roll each truffle through the coating so that it is completely covered. Place it on parchment paper.

Serve at room temperature.

Luscious Chocolate Truffles

These little delights are packed with flavor. Use any coating of your choice to make them even better.

Ingredients

515 g semisweet chocolate chips
385 ml sweetened condensed milk
15 ml vanilla extract

Directions

Melt chocolate chips with sweetened condensed milk in a large saucepan. Stir to keep it smooth.

Remove the chocolate mixture from heat and add vanilla. Pour the mixture into a bowl. Allow to chill for a few hours to become firm.

Use your hands to roll the chocolate mixture into small balls. Coat them in an ingredient of your choosing.

Store in the refrigerator, but allow them to warm to room temperature before serving.

Chocolate Truffles

This is another easy recipe that can be adapted to fit your tastes.

Ingredients

226 g semisweet or bittersweet chocolate, cut into small pieces

118 ml heavy whipping cream

29 g unsalted butter

Directions

Bring cream and butter to a boil over medium heat. Pour the mixture over the chopped chocolate. Allow it to stand before stirring to make it smooth.

Add any liquor or flavoring.

Cover and allow to chill overnight.

Place ingredients for coatings on a plate. Scoop a small amount of the chocolate mixture and roll it through the coating. Place on parchment paper and place in the refrigerator. Allow truffles to warm to room temperature before serving.

White Chocolate Truffles

These truffles are perfect for those that don't want the slight bitter flavor that can come with dark chocolate desserts. They are still rich and creamy but have a milder flavor.

Ingredients

101 ml heavy cream, plus an additional 30 ml
14 g unsalted butter
227 g white chocolate, chopped into small pieces
75 g flaked coconut

Directions

Bring heavy cream to a simmer in a saucepan. Add butter, and stir it until it has melted.

Add chocolate to the cream mixture and stir until it is completely smooth.

Remove the mixture from heat and pour it into a bowl. Cover it and allow it to chill in the refrigerator for at least 2 hours.

Roll the firm mixture into small balls. Place the coconut on a plate, and roll the truffles until they are completely coated.

Easy Chocolate Cookie Truffles

These chocolate truffles will be a hit with children. Serve them at your next birthday party or school gathering.

Ingredients

448 g chocolate sandwich cookies, divided

224 g cream cheese, softened

454 g semisweet baking chocolate, melted

Directions

Crush several of the cookies into fine crumbs using a rolling pin, and set them aside for later. Crush the remaining cookies and place them in a bowl. Mix the crumbs with cream cheese, and roll the mixture into small balls.

Dip the balls in melted chocolate and place them on wax paper. Roll them in remaining cookie crumbs. Allow to firm in the refrigerator for at least one hour.

Chocolate Covered Strawberries

Nothing sparks love faster than food, and of course nothing sets off those fireworks faster than plump luscious strawberries drenched in chocolate. A perfect treat for romance, but cute enough for a simple gift, these **chocolate coated strawberries** will be suited up for that special someone.

Divine Chocolate Coated Strawberries

These strawberries are perfect for parties. Set them on a colorful platter for a treat that all your guests will enjoy.

Ingredients

360 g white baking chips
14 g shortening
18 large strawberries with leaves
90 g semisweet chocolate chips
5 g shortening

Directions

Cover cookie sheet with waxed paper. Heat white baking chips and 14 g shortening in a saucepan over low heat, stirring constantly until chips are melted.

Rinse strawberries with cool water just before you are ready to use them, and pat dry with paper towels

For each strawberry, poke a fork or toothpick into stem end, and dip three-fourths of the way into the melted chips, leaving the top of the strawberry and leaves uncoated. Place on a wax paper-covered cookie sheet.

Heat semisweet chocolate chips and 5 g shortening in small saucepan over low heat, stirring constantly until chocolate chips are melted.

Drizzle the melted semisweet chocolate over the dipped strawberries, using a small spoon. Refrigerate uncovered about 30 minutes or until coating is set.

Chocolate Covered Strawberries

This recipe is the perfect one to use when you need a special treat in a hurry.

Ingredients

360 g white baking chips
170 g chopped semisweet chocolate
85 g chopped white chocolate
454 g strawberries with stems, washed and dried very well

Directions

Put the semisweet and white chocolates into 2 separate heatproof medium bowls. Fill 2 medium saucepans with a couple inches of water and bring to a simmer over medium heat. Turn off the heat; set the bowls of chocolate over the water to melt stirring constantly.

Once the chocolates are melted and smooth, remove from the heat. Line a cookie sheet with parchment or waxed paper. Holding the strawberry by the stem, dip the fruit into the dark chocolate, lift and twist slightly, letting any excess chocolate fall back into the bowl. Set strawberries on the parchment paper. Repeat with the rest of the strawberries.

Dip a fork in the white chocolate and drizzle the white chocolate over the dipped strawberries.

Set the strawberries aside until the chocolate sets, about 30 minutes.

Creamy Chocolate Covered Strawberries

The addition of orange liquor and heavy cream makes these strawberries positively sinful.

Ingredients

170 g sweet chocolate

44 ml heavy cream

10 ml orange flavored liquor

14 g softened, unsalted butter

454 g fresh strawberries, with stems attached

Directions

Place sweet chocolate in the top of a double boiler and set over hot water while stirring to melt the chocolate.

Add the cream, liquor, and butter and heat the mixture, stirring until smooth

Dip the strawberries in chocolate. Place on a wax paper lined dish and place in refrigerator until ready to serve.

Chocolate Covered Strawberries (2)

The milk chocolate used for these chocolate covered strawberries makes them a scrumptious dessert.

Ingredients

454 g milk chocolate chips
28 g shortening
454 g fresh strawberries with leaves

Directions

Insert toothpicks into the tops of the strawberries.

In a double boiler, melt the chocolate and shortening, stirring occasionally until smooth.

Holding them by the toothpicks, dip the strawberries into the chocolate mixture.

Turn the strawberries upside down and insert the toothpick into Styrofoam for the chocolate to cool.

www.ingramcontent.com/pod-product-compliance
Lightning Source LLC
Chambersburg PA
CBHW071439070526
44578CB00001B/147